The Creative Marriage

The Creative Marriage

THE ART OF KEEPING YOUR LOVE ALIVE

ED & LISA YOUNG

Creality Publishing
Dallas, Texas

Published in Dallas, Texas, by Creality Publishing.

All Scripture quotations, unless otherwise noted, are taken from The Holy Bible, New International Version (North
American Edition), copyright © 1973, 1978, 1984 by the International Bible Society. Used by permission of Zondervan
Publishing House. Scripture quotations marked (NLT) are taken from the Holy Bible, New Living Translation,
copyright © 1996. Used by permission of Tyndale House Publishers, Inc., Wheaton, Illinois 60189. All rights reserved.
Scripture quotations marked (NKJV) are taken from the New King James Version, copyright © 1979, 1980, 1982. Used
by permission of Thomas Nelson, Inc., Nashville, Tennessee. All rights reserved. Scripture quotations marked (NASB)
are taken from the New American Standard Bible, copyright © The Lockman Foundation 1960, 1962, 1963, 1968,
1971, 1972, 1973, 1975, 1977. Used by permission. Scripture quotations marked (TLB) are taken from The Living
Bible, copyright © 1971. Used by permission of Tyndale House Publishers, Inc., Wheaton, Illinois 60189. All rights
reserved.

Any emphases or parenthetical comments within Scripture are the author's own.

ISBN 0-9725813-0-8
Revised and expanded 4th printing of previous title:
The Creative Marriage, Taking Innovative Action Toward Qualitative Growth.

This book is dedicated to my lovely wife of twenty-four years,
who has been and will always be my constant companion, my lover,
my friend. Any insights I have learned and share in this book are due,
in large part, to her leadership, heart and compassion over our life's
journey together. Thank you, Lisa, for committing daily to the vows
we shared with each other more than two decades ago.

ACKNOWLEDGEMENTS

Thank you to Cliff McNeely for your many hours of work in the writing and editing process. Thanks, also, to Andy Boyd and Chris McGregor who assisted Cliff in various aspects of this project.

Thanks to Jason Acker of Acker Design for your incredible design work on the cover and the inside formatting of the book.

Many thanks to the incredibly supportive people at Fellowship Church for allowing me to teach you each week and, more importantly, for allowing me to learn so much in return.

To my Mom and Dad, I offer my undying gratitude for modeling the kind of godly marriage that I write about in this book.

And, to the one to whom I've dedicated this book, Lisa Young, and my four children, LeeBeth, E.J., Landra, and Laurie, thank you for your constant encouragement, love, and grace in my life.

CONTENTS

INTRODUCTION

The title of this book is *The Creative Marriage*. Why creativity? Over the last twenty years of my marriage and ministry, I have endeavored to make creativity a part of everything I do in life. Along the way, I have discovered that all of us are creative beings. We are creative because we are made in the image of our creative Creator. Thus, creativity should transcend every area of our lives, especially our marriages.

We need marital creativity because God invented marriage. Genesis 2:24 reveals God's plan from the very beginning, "For this reason a man will leave his father and mother and be united to his wife and they will become one flesh." God thought up marriage. It was His idea; He started the program.

We also need marital creativity because Jesus modeled it. The New Testament calls Christ the bridegroom and refers to the church as the bride. God tells husbands to love their wives like Christ loved the church.

How much did Christ love the church? Ephesians 5:25 says, "Christ loved the church and gave Himself up for her."

He gave his life for her. We didn't deserve it—there is nothing you or I can do to merit what Jesus did for us—but with a self-sacrificing love, a holy love, a pursuing love, Christ gave his life for his bride.

Husbands, if you loved your wife like Christ loved the church, you would have a great marriage, something special.

Finally, we need marital creativity simply because marriages need it. People like you and I need it. Your marriage is moving in one direction or another, and it takes creativity to keep that relationship moving in the right direction as you strive to meet your spouse's changing needs.

I define marital creativity as the art of keeping your love alive, and we will be expanding this definition throughout the pages of this book. Love is, first and foremost, a commitment; so in the opening chapter we will talk about the importance of committing to the marriage vows and the marital work ethic in building a foundation for a successful marriage.

The second chapter talks about communication. Guess what? Sometimes I have communication breakdowns in my marriage. How about you? The Bible talks a great deal about communication, so we'll see how we can do it in a creative way.

In the third chapter, we are going to look at how creative conflict leads to greater intimacy. I worry about people who say, "Oh, we just don't fight. We just don't argue. We never disagree." Hello, are you alive? Conflict is not necessarily a bad thing. If handled creatively and correctly, it can be a great way to strengthen your marital bonds.

The fourth chapter could easily fill up an entire book by itself. It's called "Creative Intimacy" and talks about how to creatively love your spouse in the physical domain.

The fifth chapter addresses one of the most common struggles in marriage: money. We'll take a hard look at how to creatively defend yourself and your family against the money monster.

The sixth chapter deals with the very important issue of giving your spouse priority over the kids, or about how to have a spouse-centric family. If the marriage is strong, the family will follow.

In the seventh chapter, we'll tackle the very difficult issues of divorce and remarriage. Specifically, this chapter will address the challenges of blending a family and starting over after divorce.

And then, finally, in the last chapter my wife, Lisa, and I will be answering some of the most common questions we've received about marriage.

Let me add that I believe every marriage can improve at least twenty percent because of this book, which is based on God's manual for a maximum marriage. I really believe that.

So, as you begin this book, ask God to give you the creative energy and drive you need to improve your marriage and take it to the next level. Then let Him work in your life as you make a commitment to building the creative marriage.

CHAPTER 1

A CREATIVE FOUNDATION

LAYING THE FOUNDATION FOR A
CREATIVE AND LASTING MARRIAGE

I have said it hundreds of times. At the conclusion of a wedding ceremony, I have looked into the starry eyes of the bride and groom and said, "I now pronounce you husband and wife, in the presence of God and these assembled witnesses." Then I add from the Bible, "What God has joined together, let no man separate." At this point, everything seems so perfect, so right. The man and the woman have just exchanged vows and rings and kisses. The marriage is for keeps. Right?

Well, don't respond too quickly. Once you add a few kids, a few in-laws, a few financial problems, and the humdrum of life, marriage doesn't seem so certain anymore.

Some couples tell me, "Ed, we have a great marriage. We are more in love today than we were when we walked down the aisle. Marriage is great!"

Other couples shrug their shoulders and say, "Well, it's average. It's mediocre. I'm just doing time in this prison cell of predictability." They say, "Forever? How about foreclosure? My marriage is hanging by a thread. It's in the deep weeds."

Marriage matters to God: the marriage relationship is the most important earthly relationship we have. Ninety-four percent of us will marry at least once in our lifetimes, and seventy-five percent of those who divorce will remarry within two years.

Even though marriages are failing in record numbers, millions still pursue it every single year. Marriage is the anchor of the family unit. It communicates volumes to our children. Good marriages can change our communities, our cities, our states, our nation, and even our world.

With so much at stake, it is important to go back to the very beginning of the marriage covenant, and to the vows that hold it together.

THE VALUE OF THE VOWS

Do you remember everything you said on your wedding day? "To love, honor, and cherish, in sickness and in health, in prosperity and in adversity, leaving all others to keep only with each other as long as you both shall live." That's what I'm talking about.

"Wait a minute," you exclaim, "I only said that once, and I was so terrified that I didn't even know what I was saying."

None of us truly know what we're committing to on our wedding day. If we knew all that would be involved in our marriage relationship, most of us would probably be too scared to ever get married. But that's why those marriage vows are so critical. They provide a foundation of stability for your partner. They are a solemn promise that every one of us makes, before God, a minister, our family and friends, to keep the covenant of marriage through good times and bad.

A few years ago, I accompanied Lisa to her twentieth high school reunion. As I walked into the hotel ballroom, the lights were blinking and the dance floor was packed. Videos of the glory days of high school were playing. People twenty years older, with twenty excess pounds, were still trying to shake that groove thing and still trying to "stay alive." It was also twenty times more entertaining to watch than in high school!

What was happening at this celebration? The reunion committee was attempting to bring the past into the present. They were trying to make events from twenty years ago current for today. And that is precisely what I want you to do with your vows. Take those promises that you made before God and your witnesses during your wedding and pursue them passionately in the present.

In a conversation with a very close friend of mine about marriage, he told me, "Ed, just after our honeymoon, my wife became desperately ill. She has been ill during our entire seventeen-year marriage. Nothing is normal about our marriage: intimacy is not normal, communication is not normal, sex is not normal."

Then he looked at me and said, "When I recited those vows, when I said 'in sickness and in health,' I meant it. I meant it."

When he told me his story, I prayed silently, "God, let that be me." And I hope you are willing to pray the same thing, "Let that be me." Remember: To love, honor, and cherish, in sickness and in health, in prosperity and in adversity, forever.

This is not lightweight stuff. When you said your vows, you gave your word to God. You got into a covenant deal with him. In the Old Testament, a covenant was an oath that required the spilling of an animal's blood. During the signing of this covenant, the Lord was called upon to witness the transaction. In other words, this was a significant decision. Why not take your vows from the past and bring them into the present? Make them current.

You wouldn't even think about walking out of the house in a new, trendy outfit accompanied by an old 70's hairstyle. It would be irresponsible to let your insurance premium lapse. You wouldn't consider skipping your mortgage payment. You stay current with those things, because they are priorities.

How much greater is the priority of marriage? Let me challenge you to stay current with your vows. I suggest you recite your vows to your spouse at least once a year. This would be a great way to celebrate your wedding anniversary each year. You don't have to say them word for word the way you did on your wedding day. But put the same sentiment of those vows in your own words. Tell your spouse how much you love him or her. Let your spouse know you are serious about your commitment to love them and that your marriage is not just based on flighty feelings. Remind them of your forever commitment, no matter what happens. Give them an assurance of your love, honor and faithfulness. Let them know that nothing will come between the two of you as long as you live. Bring the promises of the past into the present, pursue them passionately, and continue to move those vows into the future.

I've taken the marriage vows and put them into modern day vernacular:

> *"I commit before God and you to creatively love, honor, and respect you; to be true to you in all situations for the rest of my life."*

Why are these vows such a big deal? The vows begin, "I commit before God." We can talk about creativity until, as we say in Texas, the cows come home. We can talk about the value of the vows, but it all starts with God. We have to be on the same page with Him. Our understanding and appreciation for the marital commitment that comes from our vows flow from the commitment that God (through Christ) has already made to us. When we realize that God loves us unconditionally, it will give us the endurance to live a committed life for Christ, and the endurance necessary for a dynamic and lasting marriage.

Marital math is two becoming one. And for Christ-followers that math takes on a whole new dimension, because we have a special supernatural connection through our personal relationship with Christ. With this in place, Christ will give us the endurance and the ability to work, to create, and to keep up with our part of the vows.

MARITAL MATH IS TWO BECOMING ONE.

So when you are talking to your spouse and you have a communication breakdown, when you want to spin on your heels and walk out the door, suddenly your vows will echo in your mind. You may be able to write them even better than I did, but don't forget that it all starts with God through your personal relationship with His Son, Jesus Christ.

When you get into a conflict and you feel the temperature rising, remember the value of the vows.

When one is in the mood for sex and the other is not, remember the value of the vows.

WE HAVE A SPECIAL SUPERNATURAL CONNECTION THROUGH OUR PERSONAL RELATIONSHIP WITH CHRIST.

When you get to the end of a tough day, you're in a bad mood and want to lash out at your spouse, remember the value of your vows.

When parenting pressures begin to interfere with having a regular date night with your covenant partner, remember the value of the vows.

When sickness or financial trouble put a strain on your relationship, remember the value of the vows.

Remember...Remember...Remember!

If I am going to remember the value of the vows—to love, honor, and respect—I have to realize that living out these sacred vows takes a lot of work. A commitment to making your marriage successful requires you to roll up your sleeves and engage in grit under your fingernails type work. That's the next foundational aspect to building a creative marriage.

A TIRELESS MWE

Recently I boarded a flight to speak at a conference on the west coast. After I took my seat in coach, I started watching the other passengers board the plane. One man came on with a look on his face that clearly said he was having a bad day. He walked through First Class, looking enviously at the empty seats still there, and sat down in coach right across the aisle from me.

He was just spoiling for a fight. Shortly after the plane

had taken off, he punched the guy in front of him and told him not to lean his seat back. He craned his head to peer into the First Class cabin, where they had already started the beverage service.

Finally, when the flight attendant walked by, he said, "Excuse me, honey. I noticed some empty seats in First Class. Are there any available?"

She smiled sweetly and replied, "There are some empty seats, but there are none available for you."

The man sat there stewing. After a minute he took out his wallet and looked through some cards. The same flight attendant walked back and he said, "Miss, I have this travel agent card and I wondered if you would put me up in First Class."

She smiled again, said, "No," and kept walking.

What was happening here? This man was trying to get into First Class, but he hadn't paid the price.

The same is true in marriage. If you want to have a first class marriage, you have to pay the price. The price tag is lots of hard work, but the reward is well worth the payoff.

Great marriages maintain a tireless MWE: a Marital Work Ethic. The sad thing is we are all dialed into the desire for instant gratification that permeates our culture. If it is not quick, easy, express, overnight, or disposable, we don't want anything to do with it. We think, if it takes a lot of work, it can't be that gratifying.

Then, one day, we get married and discover that marriage

takes work, negotiation, sweat, toil, pain, and sacrifice—and that it is for keeps. Our disposable culture clashes with the permanency of the marriage relationship. No wonder so many marriages today abandon their vows and end in divorce.

Ask God to develop within your spirit a tireless Marital Work Ethic. Marriage takes work. And to carry out that work in positive and consistent ways through decades of change, it takes creativity. Therefore, we desperately need marital creativity.

We fall in love when another person meets our emotional needs. Because those needs change so much, meeting them on a daily basis takes creativity and work. My needs at twenty-one were different from my needs at thirty-one, and those are different from my needs now.

Love begins to wane when a spouse says that they don't want to meet those emotional needs anymore. And people can decide not to meet those needs for a number of reasons. Some will say, "Forget the Marital Work Ethic." Others just keep on doing the same thing they have always done—the same thing, the same way—expecting different results. Isn't that the definition of insanity?

You have to understand that doing things the same old way just won't work, because our emotional needs are moving targets. These emotional needs are met when you study your spouse. You have to really understand them if you want to meet their needs. This doesn't come easily, but is well worth the effort. Love in a marriage flourishes when both partners are working to meet the needs of the other.

You may be reading this and thinking, "Okay, Ed, it's easy for you to write about marriage. You've been married for twenty-plus years, and you have a great marriage. You're a pastor, so you have it all together. You have no idea what my marriage is like."

> LOVE IN A MARRIAGE FLOURISHES WHEN BOTH PARTNERS ARE WORKING TO MEET THE NEEDS OF THE OTHER.

Lisa and I do have a great marriage. I love Lisa more today than I did two decades ago. But I go through the same challenges, the same conflicts, the same temptations that you do. I am a human being, and you are a human being—we're in this thing together.

Marriage has taken a lot of work for Lisa and me, but the work is worth it. What I find is that couples hit a relational sticking point and don't work on the personal junk that is at the root of their problems. They simply throw in the towel, abandon their vows, and opt for a divorce. Instead of looking for creative solutions to their marital problems, they take the same junk into the next marriage, and the next marriage, and the next marriage.

Situations like this get ridiculous quickly. Deal with the junk now. Work on it now and keep on working for as long as it takes. Make a commitment before God to keep creativity in your marriage for the long haul, "God, this deal is for keeps.

I am going to make creativity and innovation permanent features in my marriage."

God is doing great things, and He wants to do even greater things in every marriage. My marriage needs improvement. Your marriage needs improvement. So let's develop and live out the value of our vows as we commit to a Marital Work Ethic. Marriage is for keeps and building it with creativity will change the course of your life and mine.

One summer, I took my family to California on a vacation. I was driving late one night at around 11:00, in a Suburban packed with our four kids plus some friends we had with us. I was talking (I talk a lot) and Lisa was giving me directions since I am directionally challenged. Suddenly, in my rear view mirror, I saw a sight that causes some people to say words under their breath that I should not utter as a pastor.

"Oh, Lisa, I'm being pulled over." I slowed down and pulled off the road. This was just after I led the youth beach retreats at our church, where several of the other pastors and I had dyed our hair platinum blonde. And it was still blonde.

The patrolman came over to the window, leaned in and said, "Sir, you were swerving a little bit, huh. Had a couple of drinks tonight?"

I replied, "Officer, I don't drink. I'm a pastor in the Dallas/ Fort Worth area."

He looked at me—specifically at the platinum blonde

hair—and said, "Right. I need to see your license, sir." I started rummaging around trying to find my license, and Lisa picked up a bottle of water, chiming in helpfully, "Look, we're drinking bottled water."

He wasn't amused. The officer looked at my driver's license, then at the car, and said, "Well, a lot of drunk drivers are on this stretch. I can see you're on your vacation and haven't been drinking. Just keep your car within the lines, okay?"

In a real sense, God is patrolling the highways of our lives, isn't He? A lot of marriages are swerving, going in this direction and that direction. And like that highway patrolman, God will pull us over, check our marriages out, and send us on our way. He'll say, "Stay between the lines. Stay within my parameters, my guardrails, my ground rules for a successful marriage."

You can have a great marriage. God wants you to have one. He is your biggest cheerleader in marriage. But first, you have to be willing to say, "I am ready to do whatever it takes to have a successful relationship with my spouse. I want to do it God's way." Having a great marriage begins with you and God.

> YOU HAVE TO BE WILLING TO SAY, "I AM READY TO DO WHATEVER IT TAKES TO HAVE A SUCCESSFUL RELATIONSHIP WITH MY SPOUSE. I WANT TO DO IT GOD'S WAY."

I know how tempting it is to think about your spouse's issues, rather than your own, when you read a book about marriage. It will be tempting to think at certain points in the book, "Ed, thank you for hitting him between the eyes. He needs that so much. Get him, Ed. Tear him from limb to limb." Or, "She's been doing that to me for the last three years. Thank you so much for saying that, Ed. I'm going to leave the book open right here on the coffee table, and maybe she'll get the idea."

Let's not do that. I don't need to think about Lisa, and she doesn't need to think about me. We need to think about our own need for change. Many of us are so obsessed with what our spouse is doing, or is not doing, or should be doing, that we forget to think about what we need to change in our own lives. Allow God to work in your heart and mind to help you discover how to make your marriage more vibrant, more alive, and more creative than ever before.

The Basics Of A Creative Foundation

• Make sure God is the center of your marriage. God created the institution of marriage and He created you. Know that He is cheering you on as you work to improve your relationship with your Him and with your spouse.

• Think about the creative potential you have been given by your creative God. Just as you use this creativity in the workplace, apply these gifts to your marriage.

• Ask God to strengthen your resolve as you recommit yourself to your vows. Pursue the vows you made in the past with passion in the present.

• Charge up your marital work ethic. Roll up your sleeves and invest in the most important relationship you will ever have outside of your relationship with Christ.

CHAPTER 2

CREATIVE COMMUNICATION

BUILDING AND BENEFITING YOUR SPOUSE
THROUGH POSITIVE COMMUNICATION

Take a couple of minutes and let the following phrases sink in:

"Do not let any unwholesome talk come out of your mouths only what is helpful in building others up according to their needs so it may benefit those who listen."

"A word fitly spoken and in due season is like apples of gold in a setting of silver."

"Everyone then should be quick to listen and slow to speak."

If you didn't recognize them, I just quoted several verses from the Bible, each centering on the topic of communication. The Bible is a treatise on speaking and listening.

Husbands and wives, think back for a second to when you were dating, when everything—especially communication—was just flowing. It seemed so easy and effortless, didn't it? Do you remember those triple-digit phone bills, the long walks, and the two of you closing down restaurants?

The moment the pastor pronounced you husband and wife, the moment he signed the marriage license, you expected communication to deepen. Didn't you? You still expected those romantic talks. You still expected the long walks. You still expected to be closing down restaurants.

But something changed, something you can't quite put your finger on. Conversation became a little tired, a little predictable, and a little stale. Maybe you moved from long walks to short errands. Maybe you stopped closing down restaurants and started using drive-through windows.

Instead of exchanging long, romantic phone conversations, you began exchanging voice mail messages. Your talks may have turned from dreams and desires, plans and promises, to one and two word sound bites. Maybe, just maybe, your communication (your talking and listening skills) aren't quite what they used to be.

What separates the great marriages from the not-so-great ones is obvious. Great marriages are made up of men and women who tenaciously tackle the task of great communication. And there are three necessary ingredients for effective communication. All you need is an active mind, a couple of ears, and a mouth. The key is to engage all of these powerful resources to interact with your spouse. You have the power to be a great communicator, but it takes work and persistence.

Great marriages don't "just happen." These marriages have dedicated husbands and wives who work at their marriage tirelessly, especially in the area of communication. It all goes back to the tireless Marital Work Ethic (MWE) we talked about earlier. And that commitment to work creatively together at regular, strategic communication must come from both partners.

Struggling marriages don't "just happen" either. Troubled relationships are a result of neglect and a poor marital work ethic. The marriage may have started out with a bang and thrived for several years, but over time marital drift came on the scene. And instead of working through these communication issues in marriage (yes, we all have them), these couples threw their hands up in surrender saying, "Well, that's just the way it is. There's nothing we can do about it." You have to fight for your marriage. You need to fight to stay close with your spouse, to communicate even when it's painful, and to use all of your creative resources to blast through barriers when your marriage is bland and your problems seem insurmountable.

No area in marriage needs innovative action, creativity, and a tireless marital work ethic like communication. It influences every other aspect of our marriage. As communication goes, so conflict resolution will go. As communication goes, so sex will go. As communication goes, so intimacy and romance will go. The list is endless.

We have a couple of options when it comes to communication. These options are revealed in Ephesians 4:29. It starts with, "Do not let any unwholesome talk come out of your mouths..." Our first option is unwholesome talk. But what exactly does that word unwholesome mean?

> AS COMMUNICATION GOES, SO CONFLICT RESOLUTION WILL GO. AS COMMUNICATION GOES, SO SEX WILL GO. AS COMMUNICATION GOES, SO INTIMACY AND ROMANCE WILL GO.

On a hot Texas day in June, I took Landra, one of my then five year old twins, fishing. We had a wonderful time catching perch at a little pond near our house.

Landra, like most children, was emotionally attached to each fish we caught and wanted to keep them all. Now, my general rule is to return the fish I catch, but I told Landra she could keep one to show her mother.

I didn't realize, however, how mischievous Landra could be. While she held one fish in her hand—the one I told her she could keep—she had also hidden another fish in the tackle box.

We drove home, and she showed the fish to everyone. Lisa,

as always, was a very proud and affirming mom. We even took a picture of the six-inch fish. After that "Kodak moment," I unloaded the truck and put the tackle box in the garage.

Push the clock forward about ten days and add some triple-degree Texas heat. Lisa looked at me one afternoon and said, "Honey, something smells awful in our garage. I think something died in there."

Since our house backs up to some woods, it was entirely possible that a small forest creature had crawled into the garage, among all the bikes and Power Wheels and roller blades, to breathe its last breath.

I'm not known for great eyesight, but I do have a great sense of smell, so I was on top of this one. "No problem, Lisa," I declared. "I will sniff it out."

I walked into the garage and put my powerful sniffer to work. As I neared the source, I thought I had detected the smell of a rotten fish. But there was no way a fish could have found its way into our garage. Right? WRONG! My nose led me to the corner where I keep my fishing supplies. The smell was coming from; you guessed it, the tackle box.

I opened up the tackle box and the stench nearly knocked me out—it was horrific! With newfound freedom, the fumes seeped under the door and crept into the house. Needless to say, Lisa was not happy.

As I was studying Ephesians 4:29, I looked up the original meaning for the word "unwholesome." It means literally:

spoiled fish. Husbands and wives, we can spoil our spouse's spirit with our words and by failing to really listen to them.

Have you ever been around a couple where you could just smell the rotten fish? You can tell they have rotting perch in their lives, because of the unwholesome talk that rolls off their tongues. They tear apart self-esteem, using phrases like, "You never," "You always," or "Do you realize how fortunate you are to be married to me?" It is unwholesome talk – spoiled fish.

That is one communication option that we have, but I hope you'll agree that it's not our best option. Spouses, we wield such power with our words because of the octane behind them. And so many times, we don't realize the damage they can do. Don't spoil your spouse's spirit. Don't put dead fish in your spouse's tackle box.

Fortunately, there is another option. Look again at Ephesians 4:29: "Do not let unwholesome talk come out of your mouths, but only what is helpful for building others up according to their needs, that it may benefit those who listen."

We can either spoil our spouse's spirit, or we can build up and benefit them through positive communication. I should say to Lisa only what is helpful for building her up, like, "I admire you for that," or "You do that so well." "No one else notices what you bring to the table, but believe me, I do and I thank you for it."

There is nothing like being energized by your spouse. A compliment from a co-worker or a friend is nice, but no one else has the power to restore you with words like your spouse.

I like the next part of the verse where it talks about building one another up "according to their needs." People who are great communicators work at it. They discern the situation and learn how to respond. They have appropriate replies, appropriate words, appropriate looks, and appropriate nods for the situation.

NO ONE ELSE HAS THE POWER TO RESTORE YOU WITH WORDS LIKE YOUR SPOUSE.

The verse ends, "that it may benefit those who listen." Some translations say it this way, "that it may give grace to those who listen." In other words, my voice box can be a vehicle for God to bless others by giving His grace to the people I talk to.

When I communicate words of love to Lisa, God can use my vocal cords to communicate His love for her, His understanding of her, His encouragement to her, and His compassion for her.

A COMMUNICATION BREAKTHROUGH

The question that begs to be answered is, how? "Sure, Ed," you may say, "I don't want to spoil my spouse's spirit. I know that I have stepped over the line; I have thrown some spoiled perch his or her way, but I want to change. How do I do it?"

Well, there are several things we can do to ramp up our learning curve, several practical steps we can take that will build and benefit our spouse. These steps are essential elements in the art of keeping the love alive in our marriage.

But before I go through these steps, there is one caveat. This is not Christianity-Lite. What I'm talking about is difficult. It is tough. It is work. But, it's worth it. I communicate for a living and I still have a long way to go in this department. If you don't believe me, ask Lisa.

I want to share with you in an open, honest and authentic way some struggles that we have gone through and some good things that we have done to help our communication. I think Lisa and I have great communication. Can we improve? Yes. I am looking forward to the twenty percent improvement rate after writing this book and so is Lisa.

TAKE AN e-BREAK

Remember that Kit-Kat candy bar commercial? "Gimme a break, gimme a break, break me off a piece of that Kit-Kat bar." What about America's favorite fast-food restaurant, McDonald's. "You deserve a break today?" I'm not a big junk food guy, but you have to love the creativity of these ad campaigns. I remember these jingles vividly, even though they came out years ago. Did you notice that both of these ads targeted the word "break?" I think they picked up on something very important. We are all going at a mile-a-minute pace. We are stressed. We pack on as much as we can—and then we add even more. How about your marriage? Ever thought of taking a break to build your marriage?

I'm not talking about loading up on sugar and trans fats. I'm talking about giving your marriage a technology break, an e-break. Have you noticed how technology can both help you and hurt you at the same time? I love technology, but I've found that it is an easy way for Lisa and I to get side-tracked from our relationship. In order for these technology breaks to be effective, they must be intentional and strategic. Don't just wait for eyestrain or carpel tunnel syndrome to set in before taking time off from the distractions of technology.

It all comes down to priorities, doesn't it? You need to set priorities and plan times off when you are giving full attention to your spouse. Most of us are so wired in, hooked up and freaked out over technology that we allow the digital world to creep in and steal precious moments from our marital relationship.

Here's a case in point. Lisa and I have a regular date night, usually once a week, but at least twice a month. On one particular night, while driving the two of us to our date destination, I had my cell phone glued to my ear. I was talking about work and dealing with church business. I had lots of big, important stuff to talk about, stuff I just had to talk about at that particular time. After all, I am the senior pastor of a large church and I have to be available 24/7, and...yada, yada, yada. The rationalization can go on and on.

After about 45 minutes of conversation, I could tell that I had messed up. I had allowed technology to take away some precious moments with my wife Lisa. As I look back on that date night, I have no idea what I business I was talking about on my cell phone. I really have no clue. But I do know I missed those precious moments of communication, because I had allowed technology to eat away at our time together.

Technology is paradoxical, isn't it? We have all these things that enhance communication: e-mail, voice mail, beepers, and cell phones. The list is limitless. Yet, these very devices oftentimes end up hurting communication with the people we care about the most.

Oh, these wonder devices have all been the driving force in our modern day business world, but their very pervasiveness in our daily lives can jam the airwaves of honest, open, and regular marital communication.

Here is what Lisa and I have done in our lives. Several times a week, we take what I call a "phone fast." We don't get up. We don't make a move toward the phone. "Well, you have caller ID. Surely you check that." No, we don't.

I discovered something awhile back: I own all of my phones. The phones don't own me. I am not obliged to answer the phone when I don't want to. We go through a phone fast for two to three hours and we spend time with our family.

We also spend time, just the two of us, talking. I have learned that you have to push a lot of these electronic devices away just to get that time in. Are you too hooked up and wired in? Could technology be taking away from your communication?

PLAY IN THE RIGHT ZONE

The next suggestion is something that I call respecting your spouse's time zone. If I am going to build and benefit my spouse, if I am going to become a great communicator with my spouse, I have to respect their time zone. Have you noticed that opposites attract? Sometimes a night owl will hook up with a morning person.

Here is what usually plays out. Let's say, for example, that the husband is a "PM person" and the wife an "AM person." Sometimes the husband will try to coerce and even shame his morning spouse into flying into his time zone: "Come to my time zone. That is when I am alert. That is when I am hitting on all cylinders. You'll love it, too. Come over here with me." Give it up. It's just not going to work, and it's also not fair to your spouse.

I am naturally a night owl and Lisa is naturally a morning person. And here is what we have come to as a compromise. We have established our own time zone. I go to bed earlier than I normally would, and she goes to bed later than she normally would. We now have our own time zone, when we are alert, geared up and ready to communicate. When the two of you find your time zone sweet spot, you'll find that your ability to communicate will be at its peak. How about you? Let me encourage you to do some time zone work?

The writer in the book of Proverbs hit this one right on the head in Proverbs 25:11: "Timely advice (or at the right time) is as lovely as golden apples in a silver basket" (NLT). Hey, wives, how would you like to get jewelry from your husband every single day? Well, this verse says you can. He can give you verbal jewelry, if he communicates at the right time in your time zone.

OBSERVE SPEED-LIMIT SIGNS

Another way to build and benefit our spouse is to observe speed-limit signs. In our helter-skelter society, we have to find ways that will allow us to slow down and exit busy boulevard. Or, for the international traveler: lose the autobahn mentality. Some of us need to recognize our own speed limits, step on the brakes, and take the off-ramp to a slower and more meaningful life. No matter how much we want to deny it, we all have limits. We are not machines, and we need to stop acting like we are.

Most of us are over-challenged, over-committed and overstimulated. We are shopping and soccering and recreating our way into oblivion. We are traveling at such high speeds that we will end up hydroplaning over the most important earthly relationship in the world, our relationship with our spouse.

And while we are driving on busy boulevard, the conversation usually goes like this:

WE ARE TRAVELING
AT SUCH HIGH SPEEDS
THAT WE WILL END UP
HYDROPLANING OVER
THE MOST IMPORTANT
EARTHLY RELATIONSHIP
IN THE WORLD, OUR
RELATIONSHIP WITH
OUR SPOUSE.

"How was your day?"
"Fine. What's for dinner?"
"I don't know."
"What time is soccer practice?"
"Six. I love you."
"I love you, too."

We get into that fast lane and we push the major things, those heartfelt conversations, and those spiritual dialogues to the shoulder of the road. Then one day, during our annual moments of introspection, we look in the rear view mirror, see wreck after wreck in our marriage and wonder what happened. What happened is that we continued to live life on busy boulevard and zoomed right past what should have mattered most to us.

Every time I speak publicly about setting priorities during one of my messages at church, people run up to me and thank me. They tell me how inspiring it is for a pastor to talk about eliminating activities in order to spend more time with his wife and kids. And then they state their intentions to change. Most of these people, however, are right back on busy boulevard after a few weeks. Talk is great, but we have to follow up our intentions with action if we are truly going to change. We have to fight. We have to be tenacious about our time. If we want great communication, we must make a daily resolve to observe our speed limits.

PURSUE RECREATIONAL COMPANIONSHIP

Marital communication has the opportunity to bloom and blossom when, as partners and friends, we discover and participate in a mutually enjoyable activity. I'm not talking about sex here. Sorry to disappoint you, guys, but at least I got your attention! Recreation is another vital ingredient for a dynamic marriage. We have to discover a mutually desirable activity where the husband and wife can just play together.

Some of you might say, "Well, we just don't have anything in common any more. We just never talk." Have you taken the time and effort to find something to do together on a regular basis where you can have fun together? Have you tried exercising together or taking an art class together? It could be skiing. It could be kickboxing. It could be power walking or jogging.

Lisa and I exercise a lot together. I can run a lot faster than Lisa and can smoke her in a race, but I don't. Do you know why? I have discovered that when we run side-by-side, we can actually communicate and enjoy each other's company. It's pretty hard to do that when you are a quarter-mile up the road! I would rather jog slower and communicate more, than jog faster and communicate less.

Conversation flourishes during these casual and recreational times together. In fact, we often talk more freely and comfortably while we jog than when we intentionally sit down and try to force the same kind of meaningful conversation.

Let me also add that watching T.V. or movies together is not the kind of recreational activity I am referring to in this section. Television tends to stifle meaningful conversation rather than foster it. I encourage you to find an active activity that forces both of you to get off the couch and fosters meaningful communication. Don't get me wrong, I enjoy watching television and going to the movies from time to time. Lisa and I will go to the movies for a quick escape from reality, but we know that this isn't a substitute for marital communication. After heading to the movies, we'll usually end up at Starbucks where we talk about the movie and the events surrounding our lives. We've found that the combination of a movie and a conversation over a cup of coffee is a wonderful way to unwind from a busy week and build up our marriage at the same time.

Recently, we kayaked across a nearby lake. You wouldn't believe how many good conversations came from that simple activity. Spending this recreational time together provides a non-threatening outlet for catching up with each other's lives, thinking about important issues, and really listening to each other.

Wives, you may not believe this. Do you know what one of your husband's biggest needs happens to be? The answer is recreational companionship. Now, I am not saying that you should spend three days in a deer blind or move to a houseboat on the lake. But I am encouraging you to find something that you enjoy together.

DO THE MATH

We can build and benefit our spouse in another way. But I warn you: this one is really going to hit close to home. Remember, husbands and wives, the "216 Principle."

Lisa and I have four children and we love them dearly. We would give our lives for our children; they are gifts from God. Recently, though, I was doing some math and I discovered that we are only going to have each child about 216 months from birth until 18 years. After that, they are off to college and on their own.

Well, 216 months pales in comparison to a lifetime. I am not married to my children. I am married to Lisa. And my marriage to her is more important than my relationship with my kids. A lot of us have that mixed up and out of focus.

Children let their needs be known rapidly. "Oh, I skinned my knee." "I got cut from the basketball team." These are 9-1-1 situations. We have to help them and love them and pat them on the back and counsel them. But parents run into trouble when they begin to revolve everything in the home around their children (see Chapter 6 on the spouse-centric home).

> I AM NOT MARRIED TO MY CHILDREN. I AM MARRIED TO LISA. AND MY MARRIAGE TO HER IS MORE IMPORTANT THAN MY RELATIONSHIP WITH MY KIDS.

Couples who do this neglect their marriage, their communication, their intimacy and romance. And, one day, they wake up after 216 months and say to their spouse, "Who in the world are you?" That's why I know it is so important for Lisa and me to make the time at least twice a month to go out on a date together, just the two of us.

"Well, Ed, you don't understand my schedule. My children have all of these athletic events and school activities...." Hey, if that is your life, it is probably too busy. Exit busy boulevard. Lose the autobahn mentality. I am all for extra-curricular activities but, parents, don't overdose on them. You have to keep your marriage a top priority. If you don't, one day you will look in that rear view mirror and wonder what went wrong.

I have talked to couples that have infants and children in preschool. They say that they would love to go out, but their children cry when they leave and they don't like babysitters. I understand where they are coming from.

I remember how hard it was to leave our infant and preschool children in the hands of a babysitter. Even these days when our children are much older, they will give Lisa and me a hard time about leaving for our date night.

But let me tell you what it teaches them, parents, when we walk out the door and go somewhere. It teaches them that the husband-wife relationship is the highest priority in the family. It teaches them that Mommy and Daddy love to spend time together. It teaches them that even though Mommy and Daddy leave, they will come back happier and stronger.

It is much better to allow your preschooler or infant to cry a little bit, than for you to spend a lifetime of remorse because you neglected your relationship with your spouse. So put into practice the 216 Principle.

After the twins were a month old, our pediatrician asked if we had gone out on a date yet. She asked if we had spent time together, just the two of us. This was great counsel, and we continue to follow it to this day.

People often ask Lisa and me about the secret to our great marriage. Granted, we have as a foundation our mutual connection with Christ. But after that, I believe, as I have already indicated, that one of the key ingredients would be the time we spend together, specifically the date night. We have to fight for it, but it is worth it. If we have invested wisely in communication and recreation with our spouse, we will be happy and ready for the empty nest at the end of those 216 months.

THE SWEET SIXTEEN

Another way to benefit our marriages and have great communication is to have an RC. I am not talking about RC Cola. I used to work with a gentleman about a decade ago by the name of RC Smith. RC was a great guy, a very encouraging person.

He would come to my office regularly and every time he talked, he would smile. He would ask how I was and then tell me that he appreciated me. He thanked me for all the work I did and for the opportunity for us to work together. And I would respond that the feeling is mutual. He did it almost every day.

One afternoon when we were talking, I asked him how he could explain his great marriage. I asked him what some of the reasons were for that. And, by the way, it is helpful for young couples to have older couples, whose marriages are based on Christ, to confide in and to learn from. He said that he and his wife, Charlotte, practiced the Sweet Sixteen every day when he came home. When I asked for elaboration, he said that they look at each other for sixteen minutes and take turns talking and listening.

This is pretty strong advice. But to do this Sweet Sixteen like RC and his wife, you have to do what we've already mentioned: get away from technology and prioritize your marital relationship above that of your kids. Taking this kind of time together right after work may not be the best time for you. That's okay. Do it in the morning or before you go to bed, whatever works best for you. It could be any time of the day, but just remember to be time zone sensitive.

Stake out your relational territory in your household as husband and wife and make a daily commitment to take time out and communicate, to share and to listen.

Most likely, if you are the wife, you are saying, "Oh, I like that." On the other hand, as a husband, you just may not get this whole Sweet Sixteen concept.

Guys, let me put it in our vernacular. Most of us watch sports interviews. Don't we? We see or hear the TV personality thrust a microphone into an athlete's face and ask him a question. Then they ask several follow up questions. In other words, they interview him.

Husbands, do the same with your spouse. Don't think about the Sweet Sixteen. Instead, interview your spouse. Come home and ask her how her day was. Then ask her several follow up questions. Don't just act like you are listening. Dive into her world. Put yourself in her shoes.

Guys, because women communicate differently than men, talking about their feelings first and then the facts, you have to ask enough questions to get past the feelings so you can connect.

Identify with what she is saying. Make eye contact. The Bible says that the eyes are the windows of our souls. Also, pay attention to how you are communicating with your body language, because your body communicates your interest more than your words. And then summarize mentally what is being said and then give it back so you can know that you have connected. All of those things are huge in communication.

Now wives, you know that guys communicate first with the facts. After you wade through all of the facts, you can get to the feelings. That is just the way it is. So, wives, do the Sweet Sixteen and, husbands, the interview.

James 1:19 says, "Everyone should be quick to listen, slow to speak, and slow to become angry." Studies indicate that seven percent of communication is with words, thirty-eight percent with tone and fifty-five percent with facial expressions. Whether these statistics are exactly accurate or not, the overall principle is evident. You can give your spouse spoiled perch by your looks: the eye roll, various facial expressions, and obvious body language.

When you are listening, you drive the conversation—the

listener does, not the talker. But when you are talking, don't enter what I refer to as "the moan zone." Too many couples just whine to each other. After a steady diet of that, you can smell the spoiled fish. We need to share the tough things, but let's not forget the good stuff, too. Let's build and benefit each other.

JUST BECAUSE

Finally, to build and benefit your spouse, give a reason-free gift every once in a while. Or you could also write a reason-free note. You won't believe what this will do.

My wife, Lisa, during her busy schedule one week, walked into our church bookstore and purchased a devotional guide just for me. It was a book written by a professional fisherman, Jimmy Houston, entitled "Hooked For Life." She did it for no reason, just because she loved me. The reason I liked it so much was that I could learn about fishing and the Bible all in one. This little gift was perfect for me and meant a lot.

Some good friends of mine told me about one husband who bought a reason-free gift for his wife, a coffee mug with "I Love You" written on it. But the gift goes on. This guy is a neat freak. He gets up at 5:30, gets dressed, and, before everybody else gets up, wipes down both cars every morning. He usually makes the coffee, and then he puts this special mug on the table for his wife to have just as soon as she gets up.

For you traditional types out there, how about those good old-fashioned, never-fail, reason-free gifts: candy and flowers? Simple thoughtfulness can have a great impact.

Don't forget about notes. With the instant access to cell phones, pagers and email, we often neglect the charm of an old fashioned, handwritten love note. One simple reason-free note can communicate volumes.

Every year, our pastoral staff takes a retreat. We spend a lot of time praying and vision casting. On one of our staff retreats at Fellowship, Pastor Owen Goff, who has been married for many years, opened up his suitcase and eight love notes fell out of his suitcase from his wife, Beverly. We kidded Owen a lot, because we were only going to be gone for four days. But we also knew deep down how special those eight love notes were to him.

We have good inspiration for giving reason-free gifts and love notes. If you peruse the pages of Scripture and see how God has communicated His love for us, you will see that God has given many gifts to us just because He loves us, most significantly the gift of His Son.

The Bible, without question, is the greatest love note ever written in human history. First John 4:19 says it best, "We love because he first loved us." Let the love example of your Creator motivate you to demonstrate the same kind of love for your spouse.

You may be thinking this advice about creative

communication is all good, but what happens when the feelings get frosty? What happens when conversation becomes combustible? What happens when tempers flare? What happens when you have the constant arguing going on?

Well, that subject is so important that I have devoted the entire next chapter to how conflict, if handled correctly and maturely, can actually help move us closer to our spouses.

The Basics of Creative Communication

• Communication is a crucial element that influences every aspect of marriage; it requires our best creative energies.

• Take daily technology breaks to improve your time together—turn the ringer off on your home phone and cell phone, turn off the T.V., stop surfing the Web and spend one-on-one time connecting with your spouse.

• Slow down your schedule, saying yes to the best and no to all the rest, so you can enjoy focused time with your partner.

• Practice the "Sweet Sixteen" with your spouse (16 minutes of uninterrupted communication per day).

• Write a "just because" note or give a "just because" gift periodically to demonstrate love for your spouse in a tangible way.

CHAPTER 3

CREATIVE CONFLICT

DEEPENING YOUR MARRIAGE RELATIONSHIP
THROUGH CONFLICT RESOLUTION

Several years ago I traveled to Las Vegas, Nevada, to see a world heavyweight championship boxing match. I arrived at the arena about three hours before the big bout began in order to watch some of the preliminary action.

I was mesmerized as I watched all of the celebrities pour into this beautiful facility. I happened to notice that right behind me was a man I recognized, the famous boxing referee, Mills Lane. Mills is a fascinating character. He has a bald head, a crooked nose and a one-of-a-kind voice. He is an appellate judge/referee who also had his own television show at one time. Being the shy and introverted guy that I am (I'm being sarcastic), I walked up to him, sat down and began to talk to him about this brutal sport.

Mills was wearing his boxing referee garb and was preparing to officiate the big fight. I found it extremely interesting to watch him at work. He brought the two trained and toned boxers into the center of the ring. Then he went over the rules.

He said, "Okay, I want a clean fight. No low blows, head butting or excessive clenching." Then he paused and looked at them. "Let's get it on!" The crowd erupted, the boxers went to their neutral corners, waited for the bell and then went toe to toe as they battled for the prize.

Marital conflict is a lot like boxing. Husbands and wives step into the ring and go toe-to-toe. They throw those verbal punches, display fancy footwork to dodge the issues, and demonstrate incredible skills of negotiation. The bottom line is that fights, arguments, spats, and brouhahas are inevitable in the realm of marriage.

There will be those times when lines are drawn in the sand and sides are taken. With tear-filled eyes of anger and hurt, unresolved conflict leads to separation. You'll find that the two of you will be hugging your respective corner of a king size mattress that suddenly seems too small.

High emotions may tempt you to put on your gloves and go a few ugly rounds with him or her in an anything-goes-fight. Head butting, low blows, excessive clenching will be the norm. During times like these, all you care about is winning by wounding your spouse.

While driving through one suburban Dallas shopping area filled with stores, coffee bars and restaurants, I couldn't help but notice a myriad of married couples around the complex. I saw some walking arm in arm window-shopping. I saw others sipping lattés. I saw others sitting on park benches watching that beautiful Texas sunset with beads of perspiration dripping off their noses.

I said to myself, "What a beautiful sight!" Husbands and wives in different stages of marital development were all enjoying one another. But I wasn't naive either. I knew intuitively that although they looked so kind and sweet on the surface, behind the Dockers and Hawaiian shirts, behind the sundresses and sandals, behind every designer outfit, these couples were sporting some serious boxing gear.

I knew that they regularly entered the ring of marital conflict, and I knew that they regularly fought over the big four that cause those spectacular fights: sex, finances, children and work.

I ask you, would a professional boxer even entertain the thought of stepping into the ring with millions at stake and a title on the line without being trained and toned? Do you think they'd enter the ring without a general knowledge of the rules that govern boxing? No.

Yet, countless husbands and wives get married and deal with conflict without any training and without any working knowledge of the general rules that should govern conflict resolution.

Not surprisingly, I want to help change that. I want to share with you some ground rules and guidelines about creative conflict resolution. These guidelines hold true in every relationship, but I want to focus specifically on the connection between a husband and a wife. Since ninety-four percent of us will get married at least once in our lifetime, you had better pay attention to these rules—even if you single and contemplating marriage.

Now, as I go through these guidelines and ground rules for creative conflict resolution, I do not want you to think for a second that I have a corner on this market. I am a fellow struggler with you. I still have a long way to go in understanding conflict resolution, but Lisa and I have applied these principles over the years and they work.

Before I dive into these seven guidelines and ground rules, I want you to think about something. Think about your last fight. You may not have had a fight in a long while, or maybe a very recent fight prompted you to buy and read this book for help.

What tactics did you use? How loud did you speak? What nonverbal signals were you giving? What issues were being batted back and forth? Were any low blows, head butts or excessive clenching involved? As you think about how you reacted, I want you to consider how you might have reacted in light of the following ground rules.

GROUND RULE #1:
Assess The Damage Prior To Launch

It is so tempting to launch verbal missiles. We love those zingers, those verbal uppercuts, don't we? Marriage is a process of collecting intimate data. Our spouse shares with us feelings, thoughts, and struggles; and we download them into our spirit.

And here is what happens. In an argument, or a conflict, when tempers are flaring and we feel that we are losing, we fire those verbal missiles, manifested often in name-calling. We compare our spouse to the dog, the cat, or some other person. Quite simply, we label our spouse. We compare. Can you believe it? We take this sensitive information that we've downloaded from them during intimate times of sharing and we use it against them.

> A WELL-AIMED VERBAL MISSILE CAN HALT FUTURE GROWTH AND DESTROY A LOT OF PREVIOUS GAINS IN A MARRIAGE.

A well-aimed verbal missile can halt future growth and destroy a lot of previous gains in a marriage. As satisfying as they might feel at the time, the tough reality is that verbal missiles never serve a good purpose. When verbal attacks are used against your spouse, it will make him or her reluctant to share the kind of intimate thoughts that make a marriage go and grow. You might win the fight, but you'll lose the marriage with this strategy.

I have had the opportunity to talk to thousands of married couples and I have never had one tell me, "Ed, that verbal missile did it. That one-liner finally changed her. When I called her that name... When I told him..." No, it does not and will not work. Assess the damage before you launch the verbal missile.

One recent study of marital conflict said that one verbal missile can tear apart and take away twenty acts of kindness. It is the one-to-twenty ratio. That's a sobering thought.

> ONE VERBAL MISSILE CAN TEAR APART AND TAKE AWAY TWENTY ACTS OF KINDNESS.

I am a health nut, but my favorite candy bar is a Kit Kat® bar. During one of my Sunday messages, I ate a Kit Kat bar and had someone time with a stopwatch how long it would take me to eat it. I have a huge mouth—my dentist compares my mouth to a town house—so I have plenty of room to work. It took me twenty-three seconds to eat a Kit Kat bar, loaded with fat, sugar and calories. But it took me twenty minutes of intense aerobic activity just to work off that one little candy bar.

That is like a verbal missile. We can throw a verbal missile out in a matter of seconds, but it may take years to work it off. And sadly, oftentimes the damage, while we can repair it, leaves permanent scars. So, consider your words carefully, realizing the power they wield in your spouse's life.

GROUND RULE #2:
Wave The Banner Of Good Manners

Have you ever noticed that verbal missiles are usually fairly loud and intrusive? The gut-level explosive reactions that usually accompany a verbal fight serve not to disarm an argument, but aggravate it.

God tells us in Proverbs 15:1, "A gentle answer turns away wrath, but a harsh word stirs up anger." As you are living life together intimately, as you are sharing your heart (even in conflict), wave the banner of good manners. Why is it that we are oftentimes more considerate and kinder to our friends and acquaintances than to our spouse?

Several months ago, Lisa and I were in an argument. I was kind of raising my voice a little bit and the phone rang. Instantly, I was transformed from an angry person into a caring, compassionate pastor. "Hello? Oh, everything is great here. How are you doing? Thank you so much for calling. Oh, really? Oh, that is wonderful! Congratulations. When is it due? We will be praying for you. Thank you very much. Good bye."

And then I went right back into the argument. I had no problem extending courteous and mannered speech to my acquaintance on the phone. I should have made an even greater effort to extend courtesy to my wife, but I didn't. I blew it.

Let's say that you had a friend over for some coffee. And let's say you had just had brand new hardwood floors laid in your home. Your friend spilled the coffee and the mug shattered. What would you do? Would you say: "Hey, you idiot! You uncoordinated fool! Why did you do that? Do you know how much we paid for this new floor? You are never coming over again."

You wouldn't say that, would you? You would be gracious and say something like, "Oh, it's okay. It's all right. It will come up. Don't worry about that mug. Let's get you some fresh coffee."

Many people think that to change their marriage they need monstrous, miracle-like events to occur. Then, they believe, the ultimate marriage will happen. That is not the case. I believe that for most marriages to turn into great marriages it takes small tweaks to move the relationship to higher peaks.

Don't wait for tensions to mount and conflicts to occur before deciding you need to tone down your inflammatory rhetoric. My wife and I have discovered that the key to conflict resolution is what happens before the boxing gloves go on, when things are going smoothly.

We need to make a consistent and conscious effort on a daily basis to treat our spouse with respect and courtesy.

Begin by saying, "Thank you" or, "I appreciate what you do for me." Be ready to say a simple, "I'm sorry," when you know you've blown it. Little acts of service, like opening the door or serving a cup of coffee, can go a long way in building a relational expectation that will ease or even diffuse conflict.

The Bible is clear in Genesis 2:24 that, when a husband and wife unite with one another in marriage, they become one flesh. And in 1 Peter 3:8 we find these words given to New Testament Christians, "All of you be of one mind" (NKJV). As Christ-followers, a husband and wife are not only one flesh through marriage, but also one in Christ.

God tells us in no uncertain terms that some serious oneness should be taking place within a Christian marriage. You can't say, "Well, it's his problem," or, "It's her problem." No. It is *our* problem.

First Peter 3:8 continues, "Having compassion for one another, be tenderhearted, be courteous." The word courteous has the word court in it. When you are courteous toward your spouse, mannerly toward your spouse, you are courting them. What do you do, for example, when your spouse does a chore around the house? Hopefully your first reaction isn't "You missed a spot"? It should be words of appreciation.

Are you waving the banner of good manners? Are you being polite? Your spouse matters to God, and when you treat them with kindness and respect, you are showing that they matter to you too.

GROUND RULE #3:
Stick To The Point And Stay In The Present

It is so easy for conversation, especially heated conversation, to drift from subject to subject and completely miss the point. And if we are not careful, it can spiral and tailspin into a crash landing.

The husband walks into the kitchen. The wife spins on her heels and asks for help since the kids are driving her crazy. He replies emotionally, "You are always asking me to help. I am tired and stressed. Do you realize what kind of pressure I am under at work? You are always nagging me—just like your mother does."

The barbs escalate as her emotions heat up, "Don't bring my mother into this! How about you? You are so lazy. You sit there on the couch and channel surf all the time."

The tailspin intensifies. "Channel surf all the time? You just totally ignore me. We haven't made love in six weeks!"

"Made love? Who would want to do that with you? You wear those same stinky college gym shorts every day. You don't comb your hair and you have coffee breath."

Prepare for a crash landing, we're going down: "Oh Yeah! Well, most women would give their right arm to be married to me. I am not going to take this anymore. I'm outta here!" The door slams and a marriage disintegrates.

How did this happen? It all started with a simple household chore. The wife asked the husband for some help, and from there it, spiraled into a tailspin of communication problems. The in-laws were dragged in, threats were made, sexual frustration and divorce were mentioned.

This kind of escalation should never occur. We have to stick to the issue. If the issue is finances, have solution-driven arguments about finances. If the issue is sex, have solution-driven arguments about sex. Don't mix the issues when you are experiencing marital conflict. Look for solutions, not sucker-punches.

In the heat of the moment, be careful not to bring up every grudge, every problem you've ever had with your spouse. Stay with the issue at hand and try to resolve other issues, if and when appropriate, preferably at a later time. In this example, secondary issues quickly became accusations and personal attacks rather than an opportunity for resolution, restitution or reconciliation.

Also, stay in the present tense. Hebrews 8:12 states that God (with respect to his new covenant with Israel) will "remember their sins no more." When we bring up the past, we are doing something that God doesn't do. The evil one is the master of bringing up the past, but God's forgiveness frees us up to focus on the future.

Paul, who at one point called himself the "chief of sinners," tells us in Philippians 3:13, "But one thing I do: Forgetting what is behind and straining toward what is ahead." God does not want you to focus on your past failures or those of anyone else, especially your spouse. Love and forgiveness provide hope for the future, not fear and condemnation from the past.

Satan may be whispering to you, "Don't let him forget that mistake." "Be sure and bring up the time when she had that problem." Do as Paul asked us to do, forget what lies behind, and reach forward to what lies ahead.

One time Lisa and I were in a conflict, and I'm ashamed to say that my selfishness got the better of me. I was so desperate to win the argument that I brought up some issues from our high school dating days. I know, that was a low blow. Don't let that be you. Mature Christian love and forgiveness should compel us to stick to the present and gently deal with the issue at hand.

GROUND RULE #4:
Avoid The Subterranean Level

Too many of us are subterranean fighters. Issues of all sizes and importance arise from time to time, but many of us just bury them. Instead of dealing with them when they first surface, we go subterranean with them. This is another huge problem marriages face in conflict resolution.

Maybe it is the style of conflict that we saw modeled in

our family of origin. "Oh, everything is fine. No problem. Everything is cool. Everything is smooth." Deep inside, though, all of these unresolved issues are eating away at us. And as we continue to go subterranean with issues, all that toxic waste begins to leak into every venue and slice of our life.

Deal with issues rapidly. Deal with issues when you both are rested and can talk about them. And deal with them, the Bible says, before the sun goes down. Ephesians 4:26 cautions, "Do not let the sun go down on your anger" (NASB). Twenty-four years ago Lisa and I said that we would commit to that verse. And we have. We settle every fight before we say good night. I know it's hard to believe, but we really do.

That is why I encourage couples to pray together before they go to bed. You'll find it is very difficult to pray together if you are in an argument or in conflict. Many times Lisa and I have had to stay up almost all night resolving issues, because we don't say good night until we have ended the fight. This is a great, great tactic, husbands and wives, because it deals with all the toxic waste that is messing too many of us up.

GROUND RULE #5:
Absolutely No Psychobabble

We have read a few books, taken a few courses, or maybe we've listened to Dr. Phil; so, naturally, we think we can psychoanalyze our spouse. "Oh, you are being so obsessive-compulsive. You are such an enabler. That is classic textbook stuff." Don't even go there.

Matthew 7:3 is a verse we rarely apply to marriage because it is so convicting: "Why do you look at the speck that is in your brother's eye but do not notice the log that is in your own eye" (NASB)? Jesus was using some hyperbole here, a little Hebrew humor. Just picture it. Here is a husband with a Sequoia tree in his eye saying that his wife has a speck of dust on her contact lens.

When I am critical of Lisa or she is critical of me, we are, in fact, criticizing ourselves, because we are now one. Marriage is not a relationship of dissonance, but of harmony. In our egoistic, me-centered world, we have a tough time with the concept of harmony and oneness. The competitive one-up-manship that is so pervasive in our culture cannot and should not find its way into the marital scheme.

Our criticisms and judgments hardly ever serve to build up another person. We use them, instead, as ammunition to make ourselves look better by putting down the other person. Again, remember Ephesians 4:29. Paul says that our speech should be "helpful for building others up according to their needs, that it may benefit those who listen."

Are you measuring your words to your spouse according to what his or her needs are? Or are you spouting off selective psychobabble to meet your own perceived need to feel better and make them feel worse? Skip the psychobabble and concentrate on those crucial words, phrases and conversations that will build you both up as one flesh.

GROUND RULE #6:
Listen Up Without Winding Up

A lot of us get ready to pounce instead of listening to what our spouse is saying. We do a major league windup and cannot wait to throw the fastball at their head, oftentimes while they are still talking. When we are set to pounce, to interrupt them, it's a sure sign that we are not really listening.

When we listen, we should list things mentally to ensure we're tracking with what our spouse is saying. Really listen for the issue at hand. Once we have listed them mentally, we should give them back to the other person for clarification. Now our spouse can indicate thumbs up: yes, you got what I said; or thumbs down: no, you misunderstood.

Proverbs 18:13 cuts to the chase regarding the importance of listening, "He (or she) who answers before listening, that is his (or her) folly and his (or her) shame." If you do that, you will never communicate. Conversation, including heated conversation, is a two-way street. You may think you are having a meaningful conversation with your spouse just because you are articulating your concerns to them. But if you are failing to listen to their concerns, then you are not really conversing with them. All you're doing is lecturing them.

GROUND RULE #7
Make a You-Turn

U-turns are difficult to negotiate, especially if you drive a truck like I do. One Friday night I had the family in my truck and we were driving around looking at neighborhoods and houses. I got lost, as I typically do, and I had to make two U-turns using people's driveways. It was embarrassing.

In marriage, we need to make another kind of U-turn: a You-Turn. That's because we use the word "you" too much. You. You. You. "You always waste money." "You never talk to me." Instead, we should use "I feel" statements. "I feel that we should save more money." "I feel like we are not really communicating." It changes the whole dynamic, because revealing your feelings is the beginning of real healing in a relationship.

Paul commands us in Galatians 6:2, "Bear one another's burdens, and so fulfill the law of Christ" (NKJV). This is not an optional thing. When you train with weights, you are always encouraged to train with another person so they can spot for you. They make sure that everything is okay, help with the poundage and especially with the last two or three repetitions. A spotter is the best way to go, because that person is literally sharing the burden.

Similarly, we are to become relational spotters for our spouses. "Okay, you had a difficult run at work? I want to bear your burden." "Oh, you are feeling down about something that your father said to you? I want to bear your burden." It's about sharing and bearing the feelings of another. It removes the "I" factor and reintroduces the "we" factor.

GROUND RULE #8
Avoid The D-word

The ultimate trump card in conflict is the "D-word." Whenever a husband or wife feels really beaten down, this word will get thrown into the mix and usually ends up lighting a powder keg explosion.

Instead of working through the issues, or asking for forgiveness, the word divorce is thrown around. "I'm so sick of you. If you talk to me like this one more time, I'm going to divorce you!" That is the fastest way to end an argument but also the fastest way to head for an actual divorce.

Marriage is all about trust. It is impossible to build trust when one or both of you is threatening to dissolve a covenant that you made with each other before God.

Let me urge you never to use the D-word. Work on your own junk and seek creative solutions to your conflict. Remember, God is your biggest source of help and your biggest cheerleader when you find yourself in conflict. Ask Him for strength and help to work through your issues in a way that honors Him.

I could go on and on about these conflict resolution principles. You may have even found some others. But the bottom line is that these principles are all found in the Bible, and they revolve around a commitment by both husband and wife to deal seriously, radically and rapidly with conflict as it occurs.

THE COSMIC CONFLICT

We have been talking about human conflict so far, but many people are in a seemingly un-winnable and un-resolvable conflict that just happens to be the key to all conflict resolution. I'm talking about a conflict with God.

If this is you, you may not want to admit it, but you know deep down what I'm talking about. You have this uneasiness, this sick feeling in the pit of your stomach, knowing that one day you will have to face God and give an account of your behavior.

The Bible says that all of us have made mistakes. All of us have sinned relationally, morally and spiritually against God and other people. We have violated God's standards. God is holy. He is perfect. Yet, we have turned our backs on Him and gone our own way.

While this cosmic conflict appears to be un-winnable and un-resolvable, here is what God did to bring reconciliation. God, even though He was the violated party, took the initiative in this conflict. He commissioned His only Son to live a perfect life, to die on the cross for all of our mistakes and sins—past, present and future. And then He rose again.

If we come to a point in our lives when we apply and appropriate what God did for us through Christ, our sins are forgiven, the conflict is over and we are reconciled to God.

If you have not taken this step, you are in serious trouble. I don't care how good you are, how sweet you are, how kind you are, how much money you give away to charity or to a church; you are going to fall miserably short of God's standard of goodness. You are still going to be, at the end of your life, in conflict with this holy, all-powerful God.

> WHEN WE APPLY AND APPROPRIATE WHAT GOD DID FOR US THROUGH CHRIST,...WE ARE RECONCILED TO GOD.

Conflict resolution starts with a step of faith by saying, "Christ, I accept what You did for me and apply it to my life." Your life will never work and your marriage will never work if you have not made that decision and taken that step.

I am not talking about religion. I am not talking about a denominational affiliation. Denominations are not mentioned in the Bible. The Catholic Church is not mentioned. The Baptist church is not mentioned. The Lutheran church is not mentioned. Only a decision to accept Christ's gift by grace through faith is mentioned in the Bible (Ephesians 2:8-9). Have you taken that step? Have you made that choice?

THE MINISTRY OF RECONCILIATION

The moment that we receive Christ and what He did for us on the cross, an awesome thing happens. Second Corinthians 5:17-18 tells us, "Therefore, if anyone is in Christ he is a new creation; the old has gone, the new has come! All this is from God, who reconciled us to Himself through Christ and gave us the ministry of reconciliation." In short, our conflict with God is over because Jesus has taken care of the sin problem on our behalf.

Christ's gift to us is the key to conflict resolution in our relationships with one another. He modeled for us the ministry of reconciliation. If I did not have the ministry of reconciliation; if Lisa did not have the ministry of reconciliation, we would have a rugged marriage. It would not be very pretty. I don't even think that we would be married today if it were not for this mutual ministry in our lives.

> CHRIST'S GIFT TO US IS THE KEY TO CONFLICT RESOLUTION IN OUR RELATIONSHIPS WITH ONE ANOTHER. HE MODELED FOR US THE MINISTRY OF RECONCILIATION.

Lisa and I have a great marriage. I love her more today than I did twenty-four years ago. And the reason I am able to love her like this is the ministry of reconciliation that God has given to us. Every time we have a conflict, we look at what Christ did for us and draw on His presence in our lives to be reconciled to one another.

When Christ comes into our lives, He places the person of the Holy Spirit inside of our hearts and the Holy Spirit gives us the extra RPMs to take action in this ministry. The Holy Spirit will communicate with my spirit. He'll say, "Hey, Ed, quit being so selfish. You have been reconciled to God through Christ, something you don't deserve. Now get on the same page and reconcile with your bride." Lisa has this power operative in her life, too, and that is what makes conflict resolution so awesome for the two of us.

If you don't have the ministry of reconciliation, you are drawing on your own fallen human desires toward a ministry of retribution. Retribution and retaliation begin to take over, resulting in a barrage of damaging head butts and low blows. These blows serve no positive purpose in bringing restitution or resolution to your relationship. Without Christ, that is what our tendency is as married people. And that is the reason that nearly half of all marriages are failing right now.

When you have a conflict, take it to God. I challenge you, when you have a relational sticking point in your marriage, talk to God about it. But be prepared for His perspective. Nine times out of ten, when I bring it to God, He says that I am the one with the problem. I pray for my spouse every single day. By taking the problems to God and praying for your spouse, you are engaging in the ministry of reconciliation.

If you say that you are ready to get serious with God, you can be a great facilitator in creative conflict resolution. You can do it as you rely on the spirit of God. But it is a choice that each person has to make. In the next chapter we will be looking at intimacy, because I am confident that conflict resolution done in a biblical way opens the door to greater levels of intimacy.

The Basics of Creative Conflict

• Avoid verbal missiles that harm the deeper, intimate levels of your relationship.

• In conflict, stay on target, stay specific and stay in the present tense.

• Don't let the sun go down without resolving a conflict; deal with any issues rapidly. Stay up late and settle the issue or agree to reconcile with a future appointment.

• Settle your cosmic conflict with God and receive the reconciliation He has freely given you through Jesus Christ.

• Offer reconciliation to your spouse in the same way that God offered you the free gift of reconciliation.

CHAPTER 4

CREATIVE INTIMACY

**REMOVING THE BARRIERS AND BUILDING BRIDGES
TO A GREAT SEX LIFE IN YOUR MARRIAGE**

When you hear the word sex, what comes to mind? I know the mere mention of that word can bring a flood of thoughts and emotions. But I doubt very seriously that when you hear it you think about God or any biblical connotations. The fact is, though, you should. God fashioned us uniquely as a male or a female and pre-wired us for sexual desire; so God's Word should be our primary guide on thoughts in this area.

One morning, one of my young daughters looked up at me and said, "Dad, when you saw Mommy for the first time, did you whistle?" God has given us this wolf-whistle desire for the opposite sex. He has given us the gift of sex and He has provided a powerful setting, a valuable venue, to practice and to utilize this gift. Contrary to the cues of our culture, sex was created by God to be beautifully enjoyed in the marriage relationship. Throughout this chapter, we will be taking a look at some "sex busters" in marriage. You may be thinking, "Sex Busters? That's kind of a negative spin on sex, isn't it, Ed?" And you are right. Normally, I don't like to present the negative side of biblical principles, but in this case I decided to contrast several sex builders with an equal number of positive sex busters.

Sex is a positive thing, a good thing. It is from God and He wants us to experience great sex. He wants to build a great sex life in every marriage. However, research would show that at least a third to one-half of married couples are experiencing a moderate to major level of sexual frustration in marriage.

What are the hang-ups that serve as sex busters? Sex busters are attitudes or habits that keep us from using this God-given gift in a God-ordained way. Underlying each sex buster, on the positive flip side, are sex builders. Sex builders will help you get rid of the things that are keeping you from being the kind of mate, sexually speaking, that God wants you to be. If you want to make love regularly and creatively, you had better deal with this subject matter.

Whenever I speak on the subject of sex in church, I am amazed at how people pay attention. No one sleeps. No one drifts off into daydreams. No one counts ceiling lights. Some people might think that we should not talk about sex in the church. Whoever thinks that, though, doesn't read his or her Bible.

We should not be ashamed to talk about sex. God was not too ashamed to create sex and then put in print. The two most prominent places where we should discuss this matter are the home and the church. Historically, the church has done a pathetic job in talking about sex. Thankfully, some churches are trying to change that by getting real and talking about what God's word says about this subject.

SEX BUSTER #1:
You Don't Know What God Says About Sex

When couples are unaware of God's take on the subject, unaware of what the Bible says, it becomes a sex buster. The evil one does not want you to have the biblical knowledge, information and application principles regarding this subject. He doesn't want you to have a great sex life because, if you do, you will bond with your spouse like super glue. In addition, your sexual relationship and connection will provide a foundation for great child rearing principles. He will be defeated.

Yet, most couples are unaware of what the Scripture says about frequency, what it says about when one person is in the mood and the other is not, what it says about romance, and what it says about being innovative in the bedroom. "Wait a minute! Are you telling me that this stuff is actually in the Bible?" Yes it is. Read on to find God's answers to these common issues.

SEX BUILDER #1:
Get In Sync With Scripture

When you don't know or understand what God says about something, let me encourage you to search for the answer. This sex builder is that we have to get in sync with scriptural sexuality. There is a huge linkage between spirituality and sexuality. Couples who make time to express love to God in an authentic way make time to make love together frequently and creatively.

I have talked to numerous couples who have Christ-centered marriages, and they have wonderfully, mutually satisfying sexual relationships. Study after study shows that the most sexually satisfied people in marriage are those who pray together, those who read the Bible together and those who go to church together. God made it and they are doing sex the way He wants them to do it.

THE MOST SEXUALLY SATISFIED PEOPLE IN MARRIAGE ARE THOSE WHO PRAY TOGETHER, THOSE WHO READ THE BIBLE TOGETHER AND THOSE WHO GO TO CHURCH TOGETHER.

First Corinthians 7:3 is a foundational passage regarding God's agenda for sexuality in marriage.

"Let the husband fulfill his duty to his wife and likewise, also, the wife to her husband. The wife does not have authority over her own body, but the husband does. And likewise, also, the husband does not have authority over his own body, but the wife does" (NKJV).

This verse in 1 Corinthians talks about management, doesn't it? Your spouse is the manager over your body. He is. She is. "You are kidding me, Ed!" Look at the passage one more time, "The wife does not have authority over her own body, but the husband does. And likewise, also, the husband does not have authority over his own body, but the wife does." Are you in sync with Scripture?

SEX BUSTER #2:
You Don't Understand Your Spouse's Sex Drive

I'm going to make a fairly profound statement. Are you ready? Men and women are different. I can feel the shockwaves.

Some couples are clueless about the varying sex drives between men and women. Let's look at the man's sex drive, for instance. A man's sex drive is kind of like a sprint. In an instant, just like that, he is ready to sprint into sex.

A woman's sex drive, on the other hand, is more like a 5K run. She, more or less, jogs into sex. God has wired us up differently with unique sex drives. A husband experiences sex and from his sexual experiences flow his feelings. The wife is the polar opposite. She has to experience feelings before she can experience physical intimacy.

Here is how we mess it up; here are the problems that occur. The husband, the sprinter, approaches his wife the way he wants to be approached. He is aggressive and initiative taking and he sprints into sex.

The wife, what does she do? She approaches her husband the way she wants to be approached, with romance, with intimacy, with gentleness. She jogs into sex. So, you've got a problem and some tension going on. You have one party doing his thing his way, the other party doing her thing her way. As Keith Jackson, the famous, now retired, college football commentator used to say, "Whoa, Nelly."

SEX BUILDER #2:
Dial Into Your Spouse's Sex Drive

We are clueless about varying sex drives. So what is the sex builder? I love this sex builder. Wives and husbands who have it together dial into each other's sex drive.

Let me talk to the men first. For the most part, we desire sex more than our wives desire sex. Now this is not all the time or across the board, but it's true in most situations and circumstances. We know how it is, don't we guys? We make our best move, but she doesn't like the move because she is not in the mood. And we know that sinking feeling we have when that occurs. If you are a man, you know exactly what I'm talking about.

Dr. Willard Harley, a Christian psychologist, has a beautiful illustration that really hammers home an understanding of a man's sex drive for the women and what a man goes through when he is rejected. Imagine, husbands and wives, a stool with a glass of water sitting on it. The husband is next to the stool and the wife is next to him. The wife is immobilized. She can't get to the water. The husband is the only one who can get the water.

Here is what happens, Harley says. The wife turns to her husband, "Honey, would you please pour me a glass of water? I am getting thirsty."

The husband turns and responds, "I don't really feel like it. I am not in the mood; maybe in a couple of hours."

Hours roll by. One more time the wife turns to her husband, "Honey, I am getting thirsty. Would you please give me a glass of water?"

The husband responds, "You know, I am kind of tired. I've had a long day, okay?"

Then the wife begins to get angry. She can feel her temperature rising. She wants a glass of water really bad at this point, so she begins to demand a drink of water. "I want a glass of water. You are the only one who can give me the glass of water."

The husband looks at his wife, spins on his heels and

says, "You are not going to get any water with an attitude like that."

The husband returns to the scene about a day later and now the wife is livid. Finally, the husband says, "Okay! Here is your water. Just drink it!"

When the wife is gulping down the water, do you think she is satisfied? Do you think her thirst is really quenched? Not really. She is thinking that she is going to be thirsty again and, if she wants another drink of water, she had better watch what she says to her husband.

So goes a man's sex drive. Like water quenches a physical thirst, sex in marriage quenches his thirst in a physical, spiritual, emotional and psychological manner. But sex must be given and received with a right spirit if it is to truly satisfy those longings.

Well, now let's pick on the men. Men are so compartmentalized, so structured, that most of us are brainless concerning the overall context of the marital relationship. We are, for the most part, one-dimensional people.

While boarding an airplane not too long ago, I walked by a group of women. One of the women was reading a book entitled *All About Men*. So, I looked at her and said, "All about men, huh?"

She said, "Yeah, it's a short book."

I nearly died laughing. As I took my seat about ten rows back, I said to myself, "I'm going to put that in one of my messages." The house could be dirty. You could have just been in a major argument five minutes earlier. If you are a man, you are still likely to pat your wife on the posterior and say, "Hey, hey, hey. How about you and me head to the bedroom?"

Wives, on the other hand, are multifaceted and multidimensional. The context surrounding the sexual part of the relationship is huge for them. They have to know that everything is A-okay outside the master bedroom before everything gets A-okay between the sheets.

So what do we do about it? Yes, there are those times when the husband and wife are both in the mood, when they both want to make love. But what do you do when one is ready for it and the other is not?

Husbands, here is what you do. You slow down. Quit being a sprinter all the time and jog a little bit with your wife. It's sometimes fun to jog. Wives, don't always run so slow. Try incorporating some sprints into that 5K. When the husband is thinking about her needs and the wife is thinking about his needs, you'll have two people understanding the pace of passion. If you want to get your partner in the mood, approach him or her the way he or she wants to be approached.

HUSBANDS,...SLOW DOWN. QUIT BEING A SPRINTER ALL THE TIME AND JOG A LITTLE BIT WITH YOUR WIFE. WIVES,...TRY INCORPORATING SOME SPRINTS INTO THAT 5K.

SEX BUSTER #3:
You Have Unrealistic Ideas of Sex

Because of unrealistic portrayals of sex in novels, TV, movies, and other media, many couples have unrealistic expectations regarding sex in their real life relationships.

At Florida State University, a good friend of mine and I would watch movies together every once in a while. And every time he saw something that was lame, that was a reach, he would say, "Ehhhhh, unrealistic." The first couple of times it was funny, but after the tenth time, I wanted to hit him.

Like my friend—but perhaps in a less annoying way—we need to be identifying unrealistic ideas and images regarding sexuality every time we see and hear them. Virtually everywhere we turn, in every avenue of life, we get hit with this stuff over and over again.

Take our popular, modern day romantic comedies as an example. Sex rarely, if ever, happens in real life like it does on the silver screen. A man and a woman just look at each other and five seconds later the clothes are ripped off and.... That is not the way it happens in marriage. So when you see it, just say, "Ehhhhhh, unrealistic."

If the Hollywood crowd had it down cold, then their lives wouldn't be so messed up. If you had to be buff and beautiful to have great sex, then they would have a corner on the market. But you are talking about some seriously messed up people. All you have to do is go through the checkout line at the grocery store and look at the front covers of the magazines to see that these people's lives aren't exactly perfect.

Don't measure your sexuality through the grid of movies, videos and the secular media. That is not the real story.

Let me also say something about pornography here. It has become somewhat vogue these days to bring adult videos into the bedroom. Husbands and wives rationalize this by saying that it will give them a boost in the bedroom, as they watch another couple make love. "What turns them on will turns us on" is the rationalization. I have read the research. Don't go there.

First of all, when you bring an adult video into the bedroom, you are involved in lusting after and being aroused by another person or persons. The excuse that you are just watching and not actually involved with someone else does not hold biblical water. Christ said that if you lust after someone in your heart, you are committing adultery.

Second of all, pornography will always get you wanting more and more. You will get addicted to the extra stimulation and will start to need it just to be aroused with your spouse.

Here's some straight-forward advice: If you are involved

with pornographic videos, throw them out and don't get another one. And, by all means, if you have reached the level of addiction, get help from a good Christian counselor or support group. Pornography has the potential to leave great marriages on the ash heap. If it is not dealt with seriously and swiftly, it will destroy the intimacy with your spouse. Do whatever it takes, now, to remove this incendiary influence from your life—before it's too late.

SEX BUILDER #3:
See Through the Secular Smoke Screen

See through the smoke screen, this secular smoke screen that distorts the realities of a biblical commitment in marriage. Run your love life through the scriptural grid and see what the Bible says about one man and one woman committed to God and to each other in the context of marriage—a man and woman who are selflessly serving one another with energy and creativity. These couples see sex as an opportunity for greater intimacy and mutual discipleship. In short, it's a win-win for these couples.

After speaking on this subject in one of our weekend worship services at Fellowship Church, one lady commented enthusiastically to my wife, Lisa, "I really enjoyed today's message. My husband and I are going to go home and do some discipleship." Amen!

SEX BUSTER #4:
You Are Trashing The Temple

This sex buster is one of my favorites, because it such an obvious issue and yet something we often overlook. Pay attention to grooming and hygiene issues.

As men, many of us after we're married say, "Hey, I've got my spouse. I can lose the look and gain the weight. I can go on a hygiene hiatus, man. But you should have seen me when I was dating her, though. Back then, I was looking good!"

Some are so pitiful at this hygiene stuff that they are still walking around with that high school jock look, complete with the same old gym shorts, tattered tank top, and rough, unshaven face. He's thinking, "Hey, baby! I've still got it, you know." The wife is wondering why she would even want to touch him.

Here is what the wives do. They end up wearing one of those "Not tonight, honey" nightgowns to bed. You know, the kind that screams "I gotta headache." I'm sure you know what I am talking about.

We can laugh at these humorous scenarios, but they represent a real life problem in many marriages. After we say, "I do," we often follow it up with, "I don't." "I don't need to work hard to look good for my spouse anymore." "I don't need to worry about competing for her or dating her." "I don't have to impress him any longer by taking care of my body."

Being in the ministry is something that I absolutely love. There is nothing like it. I see the good. I see the miracles of God as I witness lives being changed regularly. But I also see the other side. I see the results of sin and the devastation of relationships that go astray. And what often amazes me is the physical transformation of someone who is recently separated, divorced or involved in an extramarital affair. Talk about a transformation!

Sometimes someone who is involved in adultery will come and talk to me about it. I will look at him or her and think, "What happened to you? You have lost twenty-five pounds. You are dressing cool and have a different hairstyle. I see that you're working for it now with this other person. Why didn't you work for it with your spouse in marriage?"

I will see someone who has just gone through a divorce. She has lost forty pounds and looks like she just had a total makeover. Why didn't she do it when she was married? While there are some exceptions, and this doesn't necessarily happen across the board, I have to ask myself, "Why did you wait so long to take care of your appearance?"

On the way to the airport in another city, I was in a taxi and spotted a sign which read, "It's all about work." This should be your marital bumper sticker. Remember the MWE, the Marital Work Ethic? It takes work to deal with all of these sex busters, but it especially takes a commitment of hard work to continue to court your spouse by maintaining your physical appearance. Don't neglect the obvious: you can't keep your sex life in shape if you don't keep your body in shape.

SEX BUILDER #4:
Take Care of The Temple

This sex builder comes from 1 Corinthians 6:19: "Do you not know that your body is a temple of the Holy Spirit, who is in you, whom you have received from God" (NKJV)? Take care of the temple. If you are a Christ-follower, your body is a temple, the dwelling place of the Holy Spirit of God.

We have a saying in Texas, "Don't mess with Texas." Well, God is saying, "Don't trash the temple." I am not talking about turning into a Ken and Barbie couple or a physical obsession that can take over your life. I am saying, though, to do the best with what you have.

WHEN WE TAKE CARE OF OUR BODY, OUR TEMPLE, WE ARE EXPRESSING LOVE TO GOD AND LOVE FOR OUR SPOUSE.

Eating properly, working out, and staying as lean as possible are acts of worship to God. Romans 12:1 says to "present your bodies as living sacrifices, holy and pleasing to God." When we take care of our body, our temple, we are expressing love to God and love for our spouse.

SEX BUSTER #5:
You Are Making Excuses Instead Of Making Love

I have to mention this one because, in 1 Corinthians 7:5, the Bible just puts it in our faces. Sex Buster number five is the great refusal. You know what I am talking about. One wants it, the other says, "No, I'm tired. I'm fatigued. That's all you think about." And most of the time—no offense, wives—it is a situation where the woman is giving those responses.

Let me share with you what happens when you have a negative response to your spouse's advances. First of all, you can shame your spouse by your response. By constantly turning your spouse down, you are communicating that something must be wrong with his or her desires or that his or her needs are not legitimate. It takes a certain amount of vulnerability to ask for your sexual needs to be met, and it is embarrassing and defeating for that vulnerability to be rejected.

Secondly, you can mess up your fellowship with God. It is a sin to deprive your spouse of their sexual needs. And any sin puts a strain on your fellowship with the Lord. The marriage relationship is also a reflection of the relationship that Christ has with the Church. Because of this unique correlation, when your marriage relationship is strained, your relationship with Christ is also negatively impacted.

Thirdly, you are inviting heightened temptations for both you and your spouse. Sadly, when husbands and wives do not get what they need at home, they will go looking elsewhere for it. The potentially devastating results of the "wandering eye" are obvious.

SEX BUILDER #5:
Stop Depriving One Another

In other words, don't make excuses. Make love. "Ed, those are bold words." Those aren't my words. Let's call in the Corinthians. They were having arguments about this back in biblical times, when one was in the mood and the other not.

The Apostle Paul, inspired by the Holy Spirit, wrote in 1 Corinthians 7:5 "Stop depriving one another except by an agreement for a time, so that you may devote yourselves to prayer" (NASB). Aside from certain medical problems or health issues, the only excuse we should give is, "I'm in prayer." But you must both be in agreement.

While studying this issue, I spoke with Preston Mitchell, one of the pastors on our staff, to get his input. This was his take on the subject: "Yeah, if the husband and wife do agree to abstain for awhile, I know what the husband will be praying for: Sex!" He was kidding...sort of.

Paul continues, "And come together again lest Satan tempt

you because of your lack of self-control." I don't think the Bible is telling us that we can't ever say "no." But no should be the exception. And don't just say no. If you say no, say no with an appointment: "No, in a couple of hours," "No, tomorrow morning," "No, tomorrow night." This appointment gives the two of you something to look forward to.

A big excuse these days is, "I'm tired." But being fatigued for the most part is a mental thing. I love fishing, especially fly fishing in salt water. When I'm on a fishing trip, I can get up at 4 AM ready to fly fish. I might be physically tired, but mentally I'm ready to fly fish for tarpon. And that mental attitude helps perk my tired body up.

Too tired for sex? twenty, thirty, forty-five minutes with your partner? Mentally tell yourself, "I am having sexual intercourse with my husband, with my wife, my covenant partner. Mentally, I am going to say I am ready." You'll be amazed how your body will follow this mental commitment.

Here's a hypothetical scenario. The husband and wife are in bed and she is too tired for sex. Suddenly, the phone rings and it is her college roommate. She is transformed in the blink of an eye from a fatigued female into a fantastic phone conversationalist. "Hi, girlfriend! It is so great to talk to you. What's going on?" Her husband is thinking, "What is up my wife? How'd that happen so fast?"

It takes two to tango. If you want great conversation, you had better both be involved. If you want great romance, you had better both be taking part. If you want great sex, you had better both be aroused—mentally and physically.

"Well, Ed, are you telling me that I have to say yes a lot?" Yes, I am. That is what the Bible says. And I am not talking about an apathetic yes, "Okay, you can do it." I don't think that's what Paul had in mind. I believe that an apathetic "yes" is as much a sin before God as is refusing your partner's sexual advances.

> IT TAKES TWO TO TANGO....IF YOU WANT GREAT SEX, YOU HAD BETTER BOTH BE AROUSED—MENTALLY AND PHYSICALLY.

At this point, if you are a woman, you may be thinking, "I don't like this book at all. This guy is totally out-of-touch with reality! He is a man and, of course, he is going to say these things."

Well, let me share something with you. Lisa co-wrote this material with me, and she didn't think I was being hard enough on the women. We will come back to this topic in the last chapter, when Lisa and I will answer some of the questions we've been asked most frequently about our marriage.

SEX BUSTER #6:
You Are Letting Your Kids Block Marital Intimacy

This sex buster can be summarized in one word: Kids. Now, I believe children are gifts from God. But kids can, and will, bust up your sex life. In chapter two, we addressed the need to make your family spouse-centric. This principle is especially important as you consider how to make marital intimacy a priority in your household.

You know what KIDS stands for? Keeping Intimacy at a Distance Successfully. If you are not having a regular date night, this sex buster can rear its ugly head. If you don't have regular and enforced bed times for the children and certain areas of the house that are restricted during your "romantic hours," your intimate times will be few and far between.

SEX BUILDER #6:
Take A Romantic Getaway

The sex builder is to get on board the B-52. B stands for a break, and 52 stands for fifty-two weeks out of the year. Husbands and wives, I challenge you to take two breaks a year just for the two of you. Go away a night or two twice a year, every six months. Go away to fan the flames of your romance. Go away for intimacy. Go away for sex.

"Ed, you just don't know our finances. We can't afford that." What about camping? Maybe your family can step in to help you with the kids so you can have a little marital retreat at home. Use creativity to make it happen. It is better to pay the price now, take out a loan if you have to, than to end up relationally bankrupt later on down the road. You don't want to neglect the B52, only to one day find your covenant carpet-bombed and destroyed. Taking these breaks is worth it and will reap huge benefits in your marriage.

SEX BUSTER #7:
You Are Sharing Sacred Stuff with the Wrong People

Do not share those tidbits regarding what goes on in the bedroom with your golfing buddies, your tennis gal pals, with the person next to you at work. Don't go there.

Pay attention to the words of Hebrews 13:4, "Marriage should be honored by all and the marriage bed kept pure." Talking with a trusted Christian counselor or pastoral counselor is one thing, but that's where it needs to stop. If you blab this sacred stuff, it will take away trust from your spouse and can fan the flames of adultery.

SEX BUILDER #7:
Discuss Sex Openly With Your Spouse

The person you should be having a sex talk with is your spouse. Sit down and share your likes and dislikes, wants and desires, problems and needs. Put it on the table and deal with it.

Maybe you need to go through a book on sex like

"Restoring the Pleasure" by Drs. Cliff and Joyce Penner. You could read aloud one chapter a night together or read it separately and each of you highlights your favorite passages to discuss later. You won't believe what can happen.

If you're uncomfortable talking about sexual matters, then start slowly until you can develop a mutual comfort level for heart-to-heart sharing. The greatest thing in sex is communication, so you need to find a way to bring communication into the marriage bed.

SEX BUSTER #8 (FOR SINGLES):
You Are Dabbling In Premarital Sex

I've studied many of the major world religions over the years. And one thing I've found in each of them, without exception, is a clear teaching against premarital sex. The downside to casual sex is so obvious and damaging that the collective wisdom of all faiths agree on this point.

But regardless of what other belief systems say, there is no room for premarital sex as a single Christian person. You are committing cosmic treason before the one true God. I don't care if it is with your fiancée or someone you have known for a long time. If you are living together and sexually involved, you are sinning before God.

And when you continue to live in sin, God cannot and will not bless your present life or your future sexual life in marriage like He desires. I understand the temptation and allurement there. We convince ourselves that it's no big deal, that it's only a physical thing and won't impact our future relationship.

Premarital sex, though, is not just a casual or physical thing. It is a multi-faceted and multi-dimensional part of the total relationship. There is a spiritual, a psychological and emotional aspect to sexual intimacy.

When you involve yourself in premarital sex, you have a great chance of marrying the wrong person. Why? Sex is so powerful that it can blind your reasoning abilities. Sex bonds you together unlike anything else. You will hook up with him or her and later say, "Why in the world did I do that?" Probably, it was because you had intercourse with him or her.

If you are having sex now outside of marriage, stop. Stop! Say that you are going to unwrap the greatest gift possible for your spouse on your wedding night: your sexuality. Don't lie to yourself and don't fool yourself. God ordained sex for the marriage bed for a reason, and we need to respect the fact that, despite what we might feel, God has our best interest at heart. You need to go to Him for

> IF YOU ARE HAVING SEX NOW OUTSIDE OF MARRIAGE, STOP. STOP! SAY THAT YOU ARE GOING TO UNWRAP THE GREATEST GIFT POSSIBLE FOR YOUR SPOUSE ON YOUR WEDDING NIGHT: YOUR SEXUALITY.

strength in this area. Trust Him to meet your needs while you wait for your future spouse.

I have a close friend who lives on the West Coast. He was a college athlete and, during that time, he was very promiscuous. He became a Christian later on and got married.

After several years, his marriage was going through horrible problems and hanging by a thread. He was getting ready to do something that was so stupid that I could not believe it. Just by the grace of God and through some confrontations from his Christian friends, he and his wife sought Christian counseling.

Thankfully, they got back on track and are now doing great. But he would be the first to tell you that the reason he had those issues in marriage was because he was so promiscuous before marriage. He, so to speak, brought all of those other girls into the bedroom with his wife.

Don't do it. It is not worth it. I know that sex is fun, and that's true of all sin—at least at first. But sin not only has kicks, it has kickbacks. And the kickbacks are brutal.

SEX BUILDER #8:
Keep Yourself For The Covenant

This point is pretty self-explanatory. If you've messed up in the past or are in the process of messing up and messing around, stop now and save yourself for your spouse.

If you've been disciplined enough to keep yourself from premarital sex, don't give up. I know it's hard, the temptation can seem unbearable at times, but God will reward you for your faithfulness. Do whatever it takes to preserve this sacred act and reserve it for marriage.

Avoid tempting places and situations, like being alone together in your apartment or car. Consider some group activities where you have accountability in numbers. And follow Paul's advice to the Corinthians, "Flee from sexual immorality"(1 Corinthians 6:18). It's that simple.

When you're tempted to give in to sexual sin, run. Get out of there. Don't deceive yourself by saying, "Oh, I can handle it. I'm not going to give in to these urges." God knows how hard this area is for us, so He warns us to get out when the fire starts to get too hot.

SEX BUSTER #9:
You Are Stuck In Monotony

You've heard about a monogamous relationship, right? That's a good thing. Well, there's something out there called a monotonous marriage that is not such a good thing. In fact, it's a big time sex buster. This marriage consists of the same old, same old, rut-like relationship. You've got the same old look, wearing the same old wardrobe, talking the same old talk, stuck in the same old place, and engaged in the same old love making.

Instead of monotony, we need to model our lives and relationships after the essence of God. God is not monotonous; He is highly creative and innovative. If we know Him, live for Him and worship Him corporately and individually, we are going to have creativity in every area of our lives.

You can't do the same things the same way and expect unique results. We have to change. We have to work. We have to kick monotony out and do sex like God wants us to.

SEX BUILDER #9:
Bring Back The Romance

If you look up the word impractical in the dictionary, one of the synonyms is romantic. Don't you like that? We have to become impractical people of romance.

Guys, we need help here. Here is your challenge, men. Take a modern translation and read the Old Testament book, "The Song of Solomon." Talk about some hot stuff. It is written to husbands and wives concerning lovemaking and how to keep romance in a relationship.

Solomon was creative. He couldn't even spell monotony. Solomon made his wife earrings. Solomon wrote her poetry. Solomon paneled the master bedroom by himself with fine wood cut from the cedars of Lebanon. He took her on long walks through the forest.

What did his wife do? Did she respond to his creativity

with monotony? No, she didn't. She approached him the way he wanted to be approached. And he approached her the way she wanted to be approached.

The text reads that she danced before him in a sheer negligee. It says that Solomon took her to a biblical Bed and Breakfast. Solomon's wife took the initiative and said to him, "Solomon, let's make love outdoors. I want to show you something old and something new." I'll stop there. You can read the rest for yourself. The B-I-B-L-E, that's the book for me!

When I opened this chapter, I asked what you think about when you hear the word sex. It is my prayer that from now on you will think about God and the biblical connotations Lisa and I have outlined in this chapter. We want you to do sex His way, within His parameters and use this amazing gift the way He desires. Thank God for that wolf whistle desire for the opposite sex. Let's build great sex into our marriage by following these sex builders and eliminating those sex busters. Have fun!

The Basics of Creative Intimacy

• Look at sex the way God intended, taking cues from Scripture rather than our culture.

• Get in sync with your spouse's sex drive and talk openly about your sex life.

• Take care of your body as an act of worship to God and out of honor and respect for your partner.

• Implement creative date nights and take your B-52 getaways to fan the romantic flames of your relationship.

• If you are single, make a commitment to save sex for the marriage bed. Unwrap the greatest gift you can give your spouse on your wedding night.

CHAPTER 5

CREATIVE FINANCES

**DEFENDING YOUR MARRIAGE
AGAINST THE MONEY MONSTER**

Like most young married couples, Lisa and I spent our first years together in an apartment. Three years after we added a couple of dogs to our family (one a 140-pound Rottwewiler, and the other a 70-pound mutt), we decided it was time to look for a house.

We searched throughout the Houston city limits and found a 35-year-old home. We bought the house because it had a big back yard, and because we could fix it up over time. And sure enough, we lived there for several years.

I'll never forget the first time we ever decided to do yard work. I don't really like yard work that much, so Lisa had to coax me to get out of the house and into the backyard.

There was an old tree house in the left portion of our backyard that was in a pretty sorry condition. Not paying much attention to this eyesore, I started the mower and began to mow the lawn.

In the midst of mowing some pretty nice lines through our lawn, it happened. I found myself surrounded by dozens of bees and was stung three times. I am talking about major league stings. To make matters worse, I am allergic to bees. Needless to say, I began to dance and jump around like I was auditioning for soul train or something. I ran inside and said, "Lisa, bees ... everywhere ... stung ... ouch ... allergic ... ouch!"

With all the compassion in the world she said, "Honey, you probably just got stung a couple of times. Maybe it was just a random thing. Go back and keep mowing the lawn."

Like a good husband, I went back and cranked the mower again. This time the dogs start yelping and rolling around on the lawn. The bees had found a new target, my two poor dogs. There were bees all over them. I ran inside again, "Lisa, more bees. Dogs got stung. This is a major ordeal! I have an idea. Why don't you go back outside, Lisa, and you start the mower up and maybe we'll find the source of these bees."

I dressed up my lovely wife in a sweatshirt, pants and hat. She looked pretty good. The only things you could see were her eyes. She walked out and, when she cranked the mower, a swarm of angry bumblebees leapt out of this old, dilapidated tree house and began to attack Lisa. Big surprise, right? Although she was impervious to the stings because of all the protective clothing she had on, she was running around and the dogs were yelping again.

She finally charged the house. I opened the door from

the safety of our home and she ran inside. I closed the door, but too late. About ten bees were now inside the house and were hitting the windows. We had a serious problem on our hands. After a tense battle, we finally managed to kill the ten bees that made their way into our house, but there was still the matter of the angry bees in our beautiful backyard.

Lisa got on the phone and called a man who specializes in outdoor pest control. This man was a great guy named Mr. Smith. Mr. Smith walked with a limp since he had injured it during the Vietnam War. We explained that we had an angry hive of bees in this tree house, and he advised us to just calm down and let him handle the situation. He said, "I have dealt with bees for the last fifteen years. Bees won't sting me, because I know their habits. And I have this special formula."

Mr. Smith came over and climbed a ladder so he could peer into this tree house. The bees attacked. He fell off the ladder and started rolling around. The bees were so aggressive that he sent them off to a lab at Texas A & M to see if the bees were killer bees. He told us that these bees were the nastiest ones he had seen in his fifteen year career.

It is definitely scary when you are attacked by bees. I've been there and maybe you have, too. I want to address something in this chapter, though, that is even scarier. Have you ever been stung by killer *fees*? That's right, killer fees. It doesn't matter if you make billions, millions, thousands or hundreds of dollars; if you are married—or if you are single—you are going to be attacked in one form or another by these killer fees.

Just like hunting down the source of a bee hive, the first thing we need to do to protect our finances is to discover the source of these killer fees. Gallop estimates that fifty-six percent of divorces every year in our country are due to conflict and arguments over finances. It is a major problem and a major source of conflict in marriage.

> GALLOP ESTIMATES THAT FIFTY-SIX PERCENT OF DIVORCES EVERY YEAR IN OUR COUNTRY ARE DUE TO CONFLICT AND ARGUMENTS OVER FINANCES.

When you think about killer fees, you have to think about their three-fold strategy of attack. Killer fees: 1. Sting us, 2. Immobilize us, and 3. Wreak havoc on us. To combat this attack strategy, we need to understand the following three major sources of these killer fees.

ATTACK OF THE PLASTIC PIRANHAS

The first source of attack is in the form of plastic. Do I need to explain what I am talking about? Credit cards. You get married and begin to use credit cards to buy certain "necessary" items. You know like that special blender for your kitchen and that high-definition television for your living room. When this type of spending becomes a regular habit, just watch and see what happens.

Credit cards are kind of interesting little cards. They come in pretty, shiny colors of red, white and blue, gold, and platinum. You can buy beautiful nature pictures or have your favorite college team plastered all over the card. They have our names engraved on the bottom of the card and even how long we have been card members. And they have the most prominent display case in all of our wallets.

They seem painless to use at first. In fact, when you use some cards, you get frequent flier miles and discounts on automobiles. The banking world loves for us to use credit cards. You buy something, hand the credit card to the store clerk, the clerk runs it through a computer, gives you back the card and says, "Sir, will you please sign your name right there?" You sign your name and, no problem, you have the item. Quick and painless.

As you go on your merry way, you're thinking to yourself, "Man, a credit card is the way to go. I love this little card. It's my friend." However, thirty days later, you bring the mail in and you hear a muffled gnawing sound. And you think, could there be mice or termites in our house? And then you open up the envelope and look at the bill in your hand. Yes, that persistent sound of gnawing and gnashing is the precursor of an imminent attack by the killer fees. You are being stalked by the dreaded plastic piranhas. They smell blood.

A recent television commercial advertising a particular

credit card actually warns us of this same imminent attack. Have you seen this one? A man comes home to his wife after having bought a particular item with a credit card. She asks him, "You bought this stuff with the credit card? Do you know what those interest charges are going to do to us?"

As she's saying this, a deadly mob of barbarian warriors is descending the hill toward them, ready to ravage, loot and plunder their home. The genius of the commercial is that the couple avoids the pillage, because he used one of those cards with a zero percent introductory rate. The barbarians are disappointed to have to skip their home, but are seen going after the neighbors, who recently bought something without this "special" credit card.

Don't be deceived, don't get mocked. The couple in this commercial is only delaying the inevitable. Introductory rate or not, credit cards will get you in the end, because most of us use credit cards to buy things with money we do not have.

Studies show that Americans who have credit cards spend twenty-six percent more than those who do not have credit cards. The Bible warns in Proverbs 22:7: "The borrower is servant to the lender." Money becomes a slave trader, selling us up the river to a lender who gains mastery over us.

Basically, we have two options with credit cards. And I want to challenge you to apply these options. The first option is to pay them off every month. Credit cards should be a tool of convenience, not a financial mechanism for getting now what we can't afford to pay cash for.

The second option is more drastic, but necessary to many of us. Take a giant pair of scissors and cut them up. Some of you need to get serious about this because your finances are out-of-control. Instead of having your money work for you, you are working for your money. It is literally running away from you. You have no clue where your money is, and you are overextended. You are in major league debt because of these shiny credit cards, because of the ability to purchase things so easily and painlessly with money you don't have.

It is just too easy to hand that shiny card to a cashier. This kind of transaction makes you feel like you aren't really spending. That is the reason why those of us with credit cards spend that extra 26%. It's time to wake up and face the reality of what these cards are doing to you and your family.

A couple of years ago, a financial consultant reminded me about the warning that appears on a pack of cigarettes. He said, "Ed, you know on those cigarettes there is a little Surgeon General's warning that smoking is hazardous to your health?" He said, "I think that we should put little stickers on every credit card which would read, 'Warning, overuse can be hazardous to your wealth.'" I agree with him. If you have need credit cards for some reason, fine. Just make sure that you pay them off every month. And if your finances are out-of-control, cut them up.

The Bible never tells us not to ever borrow money. I have

heard people say, "Well, the Bible says time and time again never to borrow money." What the Bible does speak against is borrowing money and not being able to pay it back. In Psalm 37:21, God has harsh words for the person who does not pay his debts: "The wicked borrow and do not repay." We should be cautious borrowers by borrowing as little as possible, only when absolutely necessary, and only when we can pay it back.

Never let debt spin out-of-control, because debt will begin to rule and run your life. And there is no kind of pressure that compares to being under the gun financially. You'll literally cringe every time you head for your mailbox. I promise you.

> THERE IS NO KIND OF PRESSURE THAT COMPARES TO BEING UNDER THE GUN FINANCIALLY.

The world talks about financial security and for good reason. Christians need to talk about and live out the principle of stewardship. Everything belongs to God. God owns the sun, the stars, our cars and our homes. We need to get it in our heads that we are managers of all the stuff that God owns. If those plastic piranhas in your wallet are attacking you, then it's time to fight back.

THE MEDIA BLITZ

Another source of the killer fees is the media. The

American Association of Advertising estimates that the average person in our society sees or hears over 7000 commercials or advertisements a day, on the radio, television, billboards, and a myriad of other places.

Advertisers hire the best producers, the best writers, and the best actors to participate in these commercials with one goal in mind: to create discontent. They want the viewer to say, "I have to have that." "I need to buy that." "I can't live without that."

Advertising is a multi-billion dollar industry, because it works. They are succeeding in creating discontent in our society, even among Christians who should know that contentment can't be purchased at a department store.

Jesus said this in Matthew 10:16, "Be as wise as serpents" (NKJV). We need to take our cue from the cunning nature of the snake. "Be as wise as serpents and harmless as doves." When you see a commercial, let me challenge you to look at the un-pictured, hidden side of the commercial.

For example, let's consider these beer commercials? Beer commercials have to be the most creative commercials going. One of the classics features this really cool guy with about three percent body fat. He drives his $70,000 shiny sports car up to this quaint little yuppie bar, and steps out.

He walks into the bar and people greet him like he's the life of the party. Beautiful women come up to him and kiss him on the cheek, and he says, "Yes, I'll have a such-

and-such beer." The bartender sets him up with this special beverage and the announcer says, "It doesn't get any better than this."

What is that commercial saying? It is saying that if we drink this particular type of beer, we can drive a $70,000 sports car, we will have three percent body fat, we will have all these beautiful women kissing us, a lot of friends and be the life of the party. Sure sounds easy enough. Maybe we should all be buying this product.

What this slick commercial is not showing you is the hidden reality of the alcohol abuse that often occurs. It doesn't show that same guy after he orders 10 of these "special drinks," and then crashes his shiny sports car into a telephone pole—or worse, another car. The commercial won't show this man when he winds up intoxicated at home, and then abuses his wife and kids. It also conveniently leaves out the health risks associated with alcohol abuse. Whenever we watch a pleasing commercial like this, train yourself to look at the dark side of what they're selling. Don't be deceived.

How about the car commercials? You will see these cars zigzagging through the Swiss Alps and you think, "Man, I've got to have that new car because it has this new sound system, it has this new braking device, it has more horse power. If I could only have that car." It is fine to drive the car, but once again, look at the un-pictured reality. I'll be the payment book will be as thick as the Bible—and I'm not talking about a small Bible either. I'm talking about the Bibles with four translations, commentary notes and 30-pages of maps! Listen again to the biblical warning. "Be as wise as serpents and harmless as doves."

THE PEER PRESSURE PRESS

A third source of the killer fees is peer pressure. I like the word peer, because it communicates a word picture of peering at each other to see what the other person has. "They have that home. They drive that car. They are members of that club. I am just as educated, I'm just as smart, and I'm just as young. I deserve it as much as they do!"

We have this never-ending cycle of the "gimmies." We compare and classify ourselves, and we think, "I have to have that." Numbing out on the tenth commandment, we rationalize our desires by telling ourselves that we deserve this or that just as much as our neighbor does. Have you ever used these excuses before?

How did this materialistic mentality take hold in our world today? America is definitely the most materialistic, money-hungry nation on the planet. Why?

Let me give you a typical example of Al, the average American child. As Al, grows up during his impressionable years, most of the conversation he hears around the breakfast table centers on money, what it can get you, what it can buy for you. He comes to the conclusion that money really does talk.

Then he sees his father climb up the corporate ladder and, because his father is climbing the ladder, he gets raises and they move across the country to a bigger house. And then he gets an even bigger house; always up scaling and living to the max of their financial means.

The little man thinks, "Well, I guess money is more important than spiritual roots, family roots or relational roots. Sounds good to me. Where do I sign up?"

And then Al, the average American child, finally grows up. He talks to his parents about college, and his parents say, "You need to go to that university and major in that subject because it will yield the highest income. Even though you might not like the field that much, you'll forget about that when you're swimming in your sparkling swimming pool."

He graduates, gets involved in a high-power career, makes a lot of money, gets married and begins to pass on, unknowingly and unwittingly, this same value system that he learned from his parents to his own children.

As an elderly man, he looks back over his life and discovers that his whole life has been focused on the pursuit of the money monster. He has been led around through life on a short leash, oblivious to this struggle. It can happen. It is real. And I see too many of Christ's followers being led around by this materialistic, money-driven mentality.

THE BUDGET BLOCKADE

How do we take care of these methods of attack? How do we fend off the plastic piranha? How do we dodge the media blitz? How do we hold up under the peer pressure press? Let me give you four strategies to fight off these three common temptations.

One repellent has been shown to be effective, time and again, against the killer fees. It is not that Raid bug spray. It is spelled B-U-D-G-E-T. I want to address the importance of a budget, because the Bible says that we should live on and follow a budget.

First, when you set a budget, pray about it with your spouse. "What, you mean I should actually pray about my money? I have never prayed about my budget." Why do we need to do this? We need to do this because everything we have comes from God, so God needs to be involved in all decisions regarding our resources.

You might say, "Well, I am a self-made man, or a self-made woman." Ok, let me ask you a question. Who gave you the drive to succeed, who gave you the initiative, and who gave you the talent? All of it came from God. He is the One who blessed you with these incredible gifts. It is because of His sovereignty and His grace that you are where you are. Never forget that.

Pray about your finances as a couple. "God, where do you want us to spend our money? What do you want us to do? Where do you want us to put limits and where do you want us to really be generous?"

Also, set some mutual goals. I think there are at least three areas for goal setting. Agree together about some goals for saving, some goals for spending and some goals for giving. Have you ever done that? A couple of times a year Lisa and I sit down and we hammer out a budget. We then live by that budget and have a good time abiding by the budget, because it's something we have agreed on together. The process is not always fun or easy, but we feel wonderful after we have gone through it. We feel good, because we know it is something that will serve us well throughout that year and over the years together.

> AGREE TOGETHER ABOUT SOME GOALS FOR SAVING, SOME GOALS FOR SPENDING AND SOME GOALS FOR GIVING.

FIRST THINGS FIRST

What kind of budget should we have? We should live by the give-give-live budget. This is a biblical budget. The give budget is setting aside, every time you get paid, at least ten percent for God's work. The Bible says that you should give it to your local house of worship. The Bible is plain about this concept. It is called tithing.

Every time I deliver a message about giving, I see those who are generous and they are kind of smiling and thinking, "Yeah, that's great, Ed. I agree with you. Preach on."

And those who don't give are saying, "Whoa, you're talking about money again? I'm going to find a church that never talks about money!"

The first thing I'd say to that person is beware, because any church that doesn't address money issues is not teaching the Bible. Jesus talked as much about money as he talked about heaven or hell. How does that strike you? The second thing I'd say is just to relax. God doesn't want you to give grudgingly or out of obligation. The truth is He doesn't need our money. He is all-powerful and totally sufficient without our help.

The Bible says that we should be cheerful givers (2 Corinthians. 9:7). If you are a cheerful giver, God is going to take care of you and He is going to bless your life. He may bless your financial situation. He may bless you with strong and vibrant relationships. He may choose to bless you with great health. God does promise to bless generous and cheerful givers throughout scripture. In Proverbs 3:9-10 we are told, "Honor the Lord by giving Him the first part of all your income" (TLB).

You see, the amount is insignificant. If you make a million dollars a month or if you make ten dollars a month, the Bible says that the first part, the best part, should go to God. Why? Does God need our money? No, God doesn't need it, but He uses money to test us and see if He really is Lord of our life. When we hoard our money, we are showing God and others that we think we are the master of our own domain.

Giving also allows you the incredible opportunity to be involved in God's eternal work in the lives of people. Jesus said that where your treasure is, your heart will be. (Matthew 6:21) If your money is going to God's work, your heart belongs to God. If your money is going to purchase more and more stuff, your heart belongs to the ad agencies.

We can look at our financial portfolios and tell what is number one in our lives. It doesn't take long at all. Is it travel? Is it clothing? Is it a home? Is it a car? Or is it the Lord Jesus Christ?

A lot of people are wondering why God doesn't bless their finances. Why doesn't God give them opportunities? Why doesn't God do this or that? Oftentimes, it can be traced back to the lack of generosity, the lack of giving to the local church.

God promises to bless those who give to His work. Look at the entire passage in Proverbs 3:9-10. "Honor the Lord by giving Him the first part of your income, and He will fill your barns (or your condos) with wheat and barley (money, new job) and overflow your wine vats (health, great relationships) with the finest wines."

God talked more about giving than any other subject in the Bible; because, when we give, we become more like Him. The first part of John 3:16 says, "For God so loved the world that He gave." As we give, we are being conformed to the character of the greatest Giver of all.

Do you have the crippling disease called cirrhosis of the *giver*? When you get paid, give the first ten percent to God. It will bless your life, your marriage, and your family in ways (financially and otherwise) that you can't even imagine.

THE PERSONAL PAYBACK

The second thing we do is give ourselves the next ten percent. So, we give the first ten percent to God and the second ten percent to ourselves. Of course, I'm talking about the biblical concept of saving money.

Have you ever seen fire ants? We have some major fire ants in Texas. They're big here, and they're everywhere. Fire ants are interesting creatures, and you would do well to just take a step back, a big step back (if you know what I mean), and watch the fire ants. Consider Proverbs 6:6 from the NLT, "Take a lesson from the ants, you lazybones. Learn from their ways and be wise!"

The wise fire ant gathers and saves stuff, but it does not have a leader, a CEO or a coach. The proverb continues, "For though they have no king to make them work, they labor hard all summer gathering food for the winter." In other words, it lives on less than it gathers and puts the rest away for a later time when the gathering will not be as easy.

I read recently that the average European saves sixteen percent of his annual income. The average Japanese man or woman saves twenty-five percent of their annual income. The average American saves four percent of their annual income. Only four percent. As Americans in a materialistic society, we need to tone down the consumerism and tune into a saving and investment mentality.

> AS AMERICANS IN A MATERIALISTIC SOCIETY, WE NEED TO TONE DOWN THE CONSUMERISM AND TUNE INTO A SAVING AND INVESTMENT MENTALITY.

As you begin to save and invest, you will learn the principle of contentment. The Bible says over and over again that when we live God's way, we will experience contentment. We should be content with the contents of our life. We need to say, "God, I want to live on a margin, so here is my budget. I'm giving my first ten percent to you and the second ten percent to myself." And then, the remaining eighty percent is what you get to enjoy. So live it up!

THE ENJOYMENT FACTOR

God loves to give you gifts and He loves to give me

gifts. Money is not the root of all kinds of evil. The Bible says that the *love* of money is. Money itself is neutral. The question is, though, do you own your money or does your money own you?

If your money has you, then you are not really enjoying it. God's plan is for us live on and enjoy the remaining eighty percent. Are you enjoying it? Proverbs 21:5 warns, "The plans of the diligent lead to profit as surely as haste (that means credit cards, impulse buying, spending because of peer pressure) leads to poverty." Enjoying your money requires diligence and the ability to master it, rather than it mastering you.

Have you ever been to K-Mart before? That is one of my favorite places to buy fishing tackle. Inevitably, whenever I'm shopping at K-Mart, there will be a blue light special. The blue light special is one of the fun and unique things about the K-Mart shopping experience. I am shopping, looking at the fishing lures, and all of a sudden this announcer comes on the loudspeaker, "We have a blue light special on aisle sixteen, on aisle sixteen. Ladies bathrobes are on sale now."

From all over the store, I see ladies turn their carts like sports cars and speed to the bathrobe section. The blue light is spinning, women are moving furiously to buy new bathrobes, even though they don't need them. They end up coming home with fourteen ladies bathrobes, just because they got caught up in impulse spending, in haste. If you spend with haste, it leads to poverty.

And don't think I'm picking on women. Guys also get caught up in impulse spending, and, when they do, it's often on a larger scale. Rather than bathrobes, they are more likely to come home with a big-ticket item like a riding lawnmower or plasma screen T.V. There's nothing wrong with buying these things if you can afford them, if they are within your give-give-live budget. Live on eighty percent and enjoy it, but live wisely and with diligence with your discretionary income.

Almost everyone has an automobile, and each of those cars, sports cars, SUVs, and trucks has a gas gauge. What if I told you to go home this afternoon, take a hammer, just smash in the gas gauge and drive with a smashed gas gauge for a year?

Would that be fun? "Whoa, I'm not sure how much I have in here. I don't know if I should floor it, ease off the pedal, or fill up the tank." You would run out of gas before you know it, because you wouldn't have any idea how much gas was left in your tank.

This would cause you to get pretty frustrated and upset, saying words you don't really mean, getting angry, kicking the dog and yelling at the kids. A lot of us spend our entire lives without a spending gauge—no perimeters, no boundaries, and just 129 easy payments away from bankruptcy and a total loss of control.

It is my prayer that you will let God's principles of budgeting—giving ten percent, saving ten percent, and then living on and enjoying the rest—be the gauge in your financial life. If you will take these biblical principles that Christ talked about more than He talked about heaven or hell and apply them, God can and will do great things in all areas of your marriage and personal life.

The Basics of Creative Finances

- Don't let credit cards enslave you and your spouse; either pay them off every month or destroy them.

- Pray and plan for a budget that will help you meet your giving, saving, and spending goals.

- Pay God His 10%.

- Pay yourself the next 10% in savings.

- Enjoy the remaining 80%!

CHAPTER 6

CREATIVE PRIORITIES

KEEPING YOUR FAMILY SPOUSE-CENTRIC
INSTEAD OF KID-CENTRIC

The statement was made early one morning in a local coffee shop. A toddler-toting mom was sitting in a comfortable chair talking to another woman. I was sitting just a few feet away, minding my own business, studying and doing some research on marriage and family issues. While sipping their morning brew, these two women were engaged in deep dialogue.

It always amazes me how women are able to share their emotions and lock in on a conversation no matter who's around. I was sitting right next to these women, but I could tell they were oblivious to me. When the conversation turned to parenting, I naturally could not help but listen in. The toddler-toting mom was talking about the challenges of childrearing and how to maintain a good marriage with her husband's busy travel schedule. The other woman, between sips of her coffee, was discussing whether she and her husband were even mature enough to have kids.

After a while, I just couldn't take it any more. I said, "Excuse me, ladies." And they turned and looked at me like, "Oh! Someone is sitting there? Someone else is here besides us?" I said, "Do you mind if I ask you a couple of questions? I'm doing some research on marriage and parenting." They said, "Sure." As I began to probe a little into their particular situations, they began to open up and share some of their concerns about marriage and family. After a while, it was time for me to head to the office, so I packed up my briefcase and headed toward the door.

As I was leaving, the toddler-toting mom turned, looked at me, and made a statement that I will not soon forget. She said, "You know, I think I'm a great mom, but not a great wife."

As I thought about that statement, it occurred to me that a lot of parents today would echo that same frustration. I think many would say, "You know, I'm getting the parental job done pretty well. But the spouse thing still needs a lot of work." In this chapter, I want to hone in on that statement made by the toddler-toting woman in the local coffee shop. I believe it is critical to understand the tension expressed in this statement if we are going to have the kind of marriages God wants us to have.

There is an important underlying question found within

this woman's statement. By expressing the frustration that she is a better parent than spouse, she is simply asking, "Should my home be a kid-centric home? Should all of the activities and all of the stuff and all of the scheduling revolve around my children? Or should my family be a spouse-centric unit where the marriage takes precedence, where the marriage is the ultimate priority? Which one do I put first?"

This kid-centric family is popular in modern American society. This funnel cloud began to take shape during the sixties and the seventies. After World War II and after the baby boom, well-meaning modern parents turned their backs on the Bible, they turned their backs on the advice from their parents, and instead, they put their stock in people like Dr. Spock. I'm not talking about the man of Star Trek fame. I'm talking about the man of permissive parenting fame.

Dr. Spock and other permissive parenting persuaders said, "The home should be a democratic institution. Everybody is equal. There's no real leader." They said, "Parents, crawl into the playpens of your rebellious toddlers, sit Indian-style, and try to reason with them." It sounded so vogue, so hip, so cool, so modern. And liberated parents everywhere bought into this philosophy, hook, line, and sinker.

There is one problem, though, with this kind of philosophy. It doesn't work. All you have to do is take a quick panoramic view at the homes, schools and playgrounds of your community to discover that this permissive parenting style has some major flaws. All you have to do is go to a restaurant with a kid-centric family to see these flaws up close. This kid-centric pattern is tempting to get into, and I've been down that road a few times myself. But here's what happens when you put your child at the center of your solar system and revolve everything around him or her.

Let's say that a young couple, who are deeply in love, get married. Then they have a few kids. The wife steps down from her number one priority—being a wife—and becomes a mom. In essence, she marries her children. Conversely, the husband steps down from his number one priority—being a husband— and marries his career. Now he chases promotions and money. For the wife to get to her husband, she has to negotiate through a maze of work responsibilities and meetings. For the husband to get to his wife, he has to negotiate around all the needs, and the greeds, of his children.

The ramifications of this shift in priorities are numerous and costly. You have marital drift taking place, as you begin to lose touch—emotionally, spiritually, and physically—with the person you married. It can seem like you are merely sharing a house as roommates, rather than sharing lives in a one-flesh relationship. You have resentment, because the children are demanding all of your time and energy and, at the same time, your basic marital needs are not being met. All of this gives way to anger, and you begin to say explosive and hurtful things to each other out of frustration. Throw an attractive neighbor or a co-worker into the mix, and you have some major marital trouble.

This funnel cloud of the kid-centric home has been picking up speed over the past several decades and is spinning out of control. Families today are cranking out rebellious, selfish, sassy, irresponsible children. And, sadly, the same funnel cloud has been leaving wrecked marriage after wrecked marriage in its wake.

This was not God's design for the family. We are to love our kids. We want the best for them. But we must understand that making our children the center of the family universe is not in their best interest, and it is certainly not in the best interest of the marriage relationship. From the very beginning in Genesis, the obvious scriptural priority in the family unit is marriage. Marriage must take priority over every relationship in the home.

I know this book is about marriage, but in order to help you understand why a spouse-centric home is best for everyone (including the children) I want to share with you my working definition of parenting.

Parenting is the process of teaching and training your children to leave.

PARENTING IS THE PROCESS OF TEACHING AND TRAINING YOUR CHILDREN TO LEAVE.

I didn't pull this definition out of thin air. It comes straight from the principles found in God's word regarding parenting. Let's pull apart this definition and look at each facet of our God-given responsibility as parents.

The teaching element comes from Deuteronomy 6:7: "You shall teach them diligently (them being the commandments of the Lord) to your sons and shall talk to them when you sit in your house, when you walk by the way, and when you lie down and when you rise up."

The training piece is found in Proverbs 22:6: "Train up a child in the way he should go. Even when he is old, he will not depart from it."

And we discover the leaving part all the way back at the very beginning in Genesis 2:24: "For this reason a man shall leave his father and mother and be joined to his wife, and they shall become one flesh."

Children are supposed to leave and parents are supposed to stay. Thus, the marriage should be at the top of the family food chain. Have you ever wondered why there are so many twenty-somethings and even thirty-somethings still living at home? It's because their families have been kid-centric for so long. They've felt the warm spotlight for so long, and have been in the starring role for so long, they don't want to leave.

The parental co-stars are doing all the work and the stars are getting all the perks. At eighteen, they say to themselves, "Hey, this is a sweet deal, baby! I get a free room, free laundry service, and incredible meals. Plus I can work, make a salary, and have a lot of money to spend." The kid-centric family funnel cloud keeps rolling along.

Have you thought about the fact that you will have approximately eighteen years with your children, but you will have the rest of your life with your spouse? You are not benefiting anyone by focusing on the kids to the detriment of your marriage relationship. If you are not parenting your children to leave and cleave, you are missing the boat with them. And if you are not nurturing your marital relationship, you are drifting away from the one person with whom you will be spending the rest of your life. You are facing the very real prospect of living out your post-parenting years in a home with a person you don't know anymore.

I'll just put it as plainly as I know how: If you want to build a mutually satisfying marriage and be a great parent at the same time, your relationship with your spouse must come first. After all, the Bible compares Christ's love for the church to a husband's love for his wife. Children aren't mentioned there. Friends are not used in the comparison. I love children and I know you do, too. But it's all about the husband and wife, because everything else in the home flows from that biblical priority.

> IF YOU WANT TO
> BUILD A MUTUALLY
> SATISFYING MARRIAGE
> AND BE A GREAT PARENT
> AT THE SAME TIME,
> YOUR RELATIONSHIP
> WITH YOUR SPOUSE
> MUST COME FIRST.

Let's look at some of the things we need to do in order

to have a spouse-centric household, because that's what God wants. In order to attain this ultimate destination for our marriages and families, there are several destinations we need to travel through. If we are going to really understand how to change our family, our community, and our culture, we must follow the right road map toward a biblical household that places the marriage relationship above our relationships with our children.

ATTENTIONVILLE

The first destination is a place called "Attentionville." Let me ask you a question: Do children need oxygen? Sure they do. But if you give them too much oxygen, it will smother them. How about attention? Do children need attention? Sure they do. If you give too much attention to them, it will smother them. Kid-centric families are in the danger zone of smothering their kids. Parents like these will say, "Oh, what do you want? What do you need? Don't cry; here's some candy. Here's some money. Where are we going to eat? You tell me."

Twenty-four hours a day, seven days a week, these parents are giving maximum attention to their kids. You may be thinking, "Oh, that's what I'm going to do for my children. That sounds good." The problem is that the marital math doesn't work when the kids are getting all of your time, attention, and emotional resources. We must balance the attention we give our children, in certain time increments, with the established priority of the marriage relationship.

Lisa and I made the choice several years ago to make our family spouse-centric, and I'll tell you how it plays out in our home. I usually arrive home by 5:30 or 6:00 pm. I walk in the door, greet the kids by giving them kisses and hugs. Then I usually proceed directly into the kitchen. Most of the time, Lisa and I will spend some time talking in the kitchen, so I'll turn and say something like this to the children, "For the next twenty or thirty minutes, don't come into the kitchen. Your mother and I are going to talk. Now, if there's bloodshed, come in. Other than that, you just go and play."

Sometimes they'll try to cry and moan, because they want my attention. But I believe this kind of routine teaches them that Mommy comes first to Daddy, and spending time with her is Daddy's priority. It also teaches them autonomy and responsibility. It teaches them how to separate and individuate. It communicates in a real life way, "Hey, I'm a part of a spouse-centric home."

I talked to a close friend of mine a while back about this whole spouse-centric idea. He said, "Ed, you know what we do? After the evening meal, my wife and I have our children clean up the mess. While they're doing that, my wife and I walk around the neighborhood and talk. Invariably, my children will say, "Can we hang with you, Mom and Dad?

Can we walk with you? Let us go, please!" He said, "We turn and say, "No. This is our time. We love you, but your Mom and Dad need some time alone together."

Don't miss the importance of this first destination. Attentionville is a place you need to travel through, not a place in which you set up camp. Our kids need us to spend a certain amount of time there everyday, in balance with the time you spend with your spouse. I'm all for children. I love to spend time with mine, but we have to do it in a scheduled manner. You don't have to set up some militaristic, ultra-strict schedule, but certain time increments must be maintained if you are going to achieve the balance of a spouse-centric household.

NIGHT-NIGHT-VILLE

There's another destination we need to travel through in order to create a spouse-centric household, and I have written a song to illustrate this special place. I'm a frustrated songwriter and singer, and I made this song up several years ago around bedtime for our four children.

Let's all go to Night-night-ville.
There we will get very still.
It's time to go to Night-night-ville.
So everyone needs to chill.

Now, this song is not that popular around our household, but Night-night-ville is the next destination we must travel through on a daily basis. "Ed, I get it. You're telling me bedtime is important. Of course, our kids go to bed every night. That's not that big of a deal." This doesn't just mean getting your kids to bed whenever they get tired or feel like going to bed. I'm referring to a structured and patterned bedtime.

Look at Deuteronomy 6:7 again: "You shall teach them diligently to your sons, and shall talk of them when you sit in your house and when you walk by the way, and when you lie down and rise up." A structured bedtime is one of the important ways that you can teach your kids about God and His word.

Set up a routine for putting your children to bed every night. You can spend time reading Bible stories and praying. Make sure it is understood that, after that, it's lights out. And here's the kicker. This established time is not for their benefit; it's for your benefit. Don't put them down when they're ready. Put them down when *you're* ready. Take a step back and ask, "Okay, how much time do we need," I'm talking about you and your spouse, "to connect at night? How much time will that take?" Then do the math.

When our twins were five and our son was eight, Lisa and I put them to bed between 7:30 and 7:45. That may sound pretty early to you—they could have stayed up later than that—but we established this time for our benefit, not theirs.

As they get older, we reevaluate their bedtime and let them stay up a little later. Even though they are getting older, they still need that structured time of rest, and we still need that time together in the evening as husband and wife.

"Well, Ed, you don't understand. I've got a teenager." So do I. To our teenager we say, "LeeBeth, you can stay up until 10:00 or 10:15, but at about 9:00 we want you to cruise to your room and hang out there until bedtime." And it shows them, once again, the priority of the spouse-centric family. It says that Mom and Dad have something special going on. It's very tempting to let your teenager set his or her own schedule, but you need to maintain control while giving them some freedom and flexibility.

Now, let's assume you've done that. You've had a few navigational errors but have finally arrived in Night-nightville. I know that this is not an easy thing, so you should be congratulated for arriving at this important family milestone. Let's say your children are in bed, your teenager is invisible in his or her room, and you and your spouse are alone together. Even with the kids in bed and no distractions, something may be keeping you from maximizing this exclusive time together. A virus has been contracted in many marriages that keeps a lot of homes from being spouse-centric.

Do you remember the infamous "Love Bug" virus that attacked computers all over the globe several years ago? The front page of USA Today reported: "FBI hunts Love-

Bug source. Damage from e-mail virus cuts across USA and worldwide. A worldwide hunt is on to find the source of the Love Bug computer virus that jammed e-mail systems Thursday from Asia to California." Well, there's another virus that's worse than the Love-Bug virus. It's the marital Love Bug virus and it's also affecting homes from Asia to California.

Here's how it plays out. It happens when you're alone, as a husband and wife, after the kids have gone to Night-night-ville. You finally have a little free time, a little quiet time, so you decide to make a few phone calls. This is one of the major ways that the Marital Love Bug can attack your home. Keep your phone calls to a minimum during this time so you can concentrate on connecting with your spouse. Lisa and I take a phone break several nights a week, by turning the ringer off and letting calls go straight to voice mail. Just turn it off. It's a great thing. Now, I'm not saying you never talk on the phone, but you need to maintain a realistic balance.

Something else that causes this virus and messes up is housework and office work done in the home. "Finally, the kids are in bed. I have some quiet time to go to my study and finish up this project, or to prepare for next weekend's message." Or, "I can finally finish dusting or cleaning the kitchen or mopping the floor." Now and then there are some exceptions, but for the most part you should not use up this quality time finishing up chores or doing work stuff. If you do, set a time limit. Make an agreement with your spouse that you will each spend an hour doing some work, and then devote the rest of the evening together.

The next way that the Marital Love Bug gets into your home is the biggest problem. This virus can contaminate your marriage through a little device called a remote control. Many, many couples spend their evenings with the television remote, all the while thinking they are spending time with each other. "We just watch TV together, Ed. That's what we do. Watching TV together is our favorite pastime." Let's be honest. When we watch television, we don't care what our spouse is doing. We are not really doing anything to connect with him or her. We're just into the sitcom or movie or news program.

Watching some television is fine, but, for the most part, it's a vast wasteland of garbage. Something powerful happens when you give your spouse priority over your television. Once you begin to really get serious about warding off the Love Bug virus by limiting your T.V. time, you will begin to make some serious eye contact with your spouse. Suddenly, especially if you are a man, you will find yourself talking to your mate in complete sentences. Imagine the possibilities, guys; there's no telling where these complete sentence might lead! I can hear the excuses already. "Oh, man, I just can't go a night without watching Fox News and ESPN." Yes, you can. Trust me; you'll thank me later.

As you consider the importance of Attentionville and Night-night-ville, consider the words of 1 Corinthians 14:40:

"But all things must be done properly and in an orderly manner." You must be committed to regular, scheduled time with your spouse or it won't happen. If you are not proactive about this, the kids will vie for all of your attention, the Marital Love Bug will bite, and you will discover one day that you have drifted apart.

DATEVILLE

Let's travel to another location, Dateville. I've been talking about this particular destination for years now, and you will find me hammering this concept over and over again throughout this book. I encourage couples to date at least twice a month. I'm referring to a date where you and your spouse go out alone.

When I have the opportunity to speak around the country to leaders or pastors, usually during a Q-and-A they'll ask me a question like this, "Ed, tell me about your personal life. What's the most important thing in your family?" I always say, "No question, the most important thing in my family is my date night with Lisa." Ten years ago, we installed a date night into our schedule, and it has revolutionized our connection. It's like an oasis, oftentimes, in the middle of the week. It's the greatest thing we've ever done for our marriage!

During one particularly busy time in our lives, Lisa and I went for about four weeks without a date night. I was doing some speaking, and we were both doing some traveling. We could sense that marital drift was beginning to take place. If you aren't having a regular, strategic date night, please begin this routine now, this very week.

IT'S LIKE AN OASIS, OFTENTIMES, IN THE MIDDLE OF THE WEEK. IT'S THE GREATEST THING WE'VE EVER DONE FOR OUR MARRIAGE!

I know you may be thinking, "Yeah, that sounds good, Ed! Sounds great in theory, but what about the real world?" I can attest to the fact that it's not just a good theory; it can be done. Don't put it off. Hire a babysitter. Just have a standing sitter for a certain night, or a certain day. If you don't want to do that, trade off with your friends. The date does not have to be at night. A good friend of mine has "day-dates" with his wife. He has a day off in the middle of the week, so they have breakfast and lunch together, and just spend time together during the day. Look at what works best for your schedule, and then be creative about making it fit.

I have to laugh, I really do, when parents give excuses like this, "You know, we would love to have a date night, we really would. But you see, our children just will not stomach a babysitter. They throw fits and tantrums and cry. And you know, Ed, for that matter, we would love to go to Fellowship Church every weekend, but they just don't like it when we leave them in the nursery or preschool or in Children's Church."

These parents may not realize it, but what they're really saying is, "Hey, we don't run the show! Our kids do! We're kid-centric. They rule. They reign. They're the stars; we're the co-stars. Oh, whatever you want, baby. Oh, don't cry!" Please, it's good to let them cry sometimes. It's good to leave them from time to time. It teaches them separation. It teaches them the priority of marriage. It teaches them that Mom and Dad always come back. This is a healthy thing.

Let me throw in something else; this is extra credit. Parents, I challenge you not to allow your children to sleep with you. Don't do that. Now, if there's an infant in the bassinet, in the same room, that's fine. If the child has gone through some traumatic situation or has had a nightmare, then every so often it's okay if he sleeps with you. I think you're making a mistake, though, if you allow that to happen every night.

When you have a family, the first step to a great sex life is establishing boundaries with your kids, "This is a special place that Mom and Dad have. This is our bed. Your bedroom is right down the hall, so you sleep there." As you begin to teach the importance of separation within the home, it helps your children when you leave them in the nursery, or Children's Church, or camp, or with grandma and grandpa. Now and again, you're going to have to fight some battles, but it is well worth it. That is just extra credit, kind of a side trip off of Dateville.

ACTIVITYVILLE

If you are beginning to feel a little convicted at this point, this next one is going to take it up a notch. You may even feel a little defensive, like I am stepping on your toes and meddling with your life. "No one's going to tell me how to raise my children! I can't believe some of the things he wrote about Attentionville, Night-nightville, and Dateville."

I learned something a long time ago about myself. Every time a man or a woman teaches the Bible and the Holy Spirit convicts me of something, I usually have that same reaction. I say, "No one's going to talk to me that way. This person doesn't have the right to tell me what to do." And usually, when I have that kind of knee-jerk reaction, it means "Ed, you need to make some changes." So, here we go to the one of the most difficult destinations.

This next destination we need to travel through is Activityville. We're burning our children out in many ways, with soccer and baseball and basketball and cheerleading and voice and dance and art classes. I'm all for extracurricular activities. I am into athletics. I value art and dance and all that good stuff. There is nothing wrong with kids being involved in competitive activities. I'm all for these things, but the keyword is balance.

A while back, my wife and I had dinner with a worldclass,

multi-sport professional athlete. Over the appetizer portion of this meal together, this man looked at Lisa and I and said, "You know, I will never let my children play children's athletics or get too involved in extracurricular activities. I want them to enjoy being kids." Now, I don't know if I'd go that far. Such a restriction is probably a bit extreme and may be driven by some negative experiences from his own childhood. But I certainly understood where he was coming from. We need to allow children to be children, and over-scheduling them can take away from that carefree, childhood experience.

I think it's good for children to play in leagues to a certain extent. Between the ages of six and eleven, however, we must be very careful about pushing them too far, too fast. Ask yourself this question: Why do I want my child to play in or to be involved in this activity? Is it because you are an F.A.A.: Frustrated All American? There's a little F.A.A. in each of us. "You know, if I hadn't blown my knee out, I would probably be in the NFL right now." No, you wouldn't. Let's just face the facts, okay? You are not in the NFL because you weren't good enough! "Well, if my voice teacher hadn't been such a snob, and if she hadn't liked Heather instead of me, I would be like Celine Dion." I'm sorry to rain on your vocal parade, but, no, you would not be Celine.

The problem with children's athletics is that adults set the leagues up, adults schedule them, and what you find is that children play for the approval of their parents. Take soccer, for instance. Have you ever gone to a little league soccer game before? During one soccer game, my son was playing goalie. E.J. was having hard time focusing at various times during the game, as little kids often do, particularly when the action was down on the other end of the field.

He was down there by himself, skipping rope, looking at flowers or pulling blades of grass. Meanwhile, I was on the sideline yelling out, "EJ, get in the game, man! Pay attention!" And then I thought, "What am I doing? He's just a little boy doing what little boys do." We have to keep a balance and take the pressure off of these kids to constantly perform and compete.

Don't misunderstand me by thinking, "Well, Ed said that our children can never play athletics or get involved in activities." I'm not saying that. It's got to be your decision before God. In Matthew 6:33, Jesus said, "But seek first his kingdom and his righteousness and all these things will be added to you."

Are you a Matthew 6:33 family? Can you keep the pace you're keeping with your current lineup of activities and sports and still be a Matthew 6:33 family? That's the balance you need to achieve as you make your way through Activityville. I can't make the call for you. You've got to make it yourself.

I hear this from parents all the time, "Oh, yeah, we love the church. We want to develop our marriage. We want to develop our relationship with Christ and be a Matthew 6:33 family.

But our kids can't go to the junior high program at the church because they have a select soccer practice every weekend. They can't get involved in the children's camp or the youth mission trip, because they already have a tournament scheduled."

You have to make the choice for your family to establish balance. The moment activities begin to encroach upon your development as a husband and wife, and especially upon your relationship with the local church, you know it's time to take the next train out of Activityville.

Remember the statement by the toddler-toting mom? "I'm a good mother, but not that great of a wife." If that statement is true for you, if it resonates with you, you need to navigate successfully through each of these destinations: Attentionville, Night-night-ville, Dateville, and Activityville. On the other hand, you may be able to say, "Ed, you know what, I really think I have a spouse-centric home." If so, I hope you will use this chapter as a reminder to keep that balance in your home. I know it has been a good refresher course for me. The pressures on the family are constant. We need to fight for our family by continuously evaluating our commitments

THE MOMENT ACTIVITIES BEGIN TO ENCROACH UPON YOUR DEVELOPMENT AS A HUSBAND AND WIFE, AND ESPECIALLY UPON YOUR RELATIONSHIP WITH THE LOCAL CHURCH, YOU KNOW IT'S TIME TO TAKE THE NEXT TRAIN OUT OF ACTIVITYVILLE.

against our priority of being a Matthew 6:33 family. When we make the decision to follow the right map toward the right destinations, we can look forward to reaching the ultimate destination of a loving and spouse-centric household.

Creative Priorities Balanced Family Test

The following quiz is designed to help you evaluate, in a practical way, how you are balancing the priorities of marriage and family. Answer each question as honestly and accurately as you can by circling the appropriate number (1-Never, 2-Sometimes, or 3-Always). Then add up all the numbers you circled to get your total score. A scoring explanation is included at the end of the quiz.

Creative Priorities Balanced Family Test

1. Do you go on a date with your spouse at least twice a month?

Never	Sometimes	Always
1	2	3

2. Do you eat dinner as a family around the dinner table at least three times per week?

Never	Sometimes	Always
1	2	3

3. Do your children sleep in their own beds (not your bed)?

Never	Sometimes	Always
1	2	3

4. Do you and your spouse have TLC (Touch, Look, Conversation) on a daily basis?

Never	Sometimes	Always
1	2	3

5. Do you get away for a weekend alone as a couple (without your kids) at least twice a year?

Never	Sometimes	Always
1	2	3

6. Do you have sexual intimacy with your spouse at least two times a week?

Never	Sometimes	Always
1	2	3

7. Do you and your spouse present a unified front when your children question your authority?

Never	Sometimes	Always
1	2	3

8. Do you have a set bedtime for your kids/teens that is consistently enforced?

Never	Sometimes	Always
1	2	3

9. Do you regularly evaluate your calendar to prevent ECA-itis (over-scheduling Extra-Curricular Activities)?

Never	Sometimes	Always
1	2	3

10. Is weekly church attendance (age-appropriate worship/ teaching) a priority for you and your children?

Never	Sometimes	Always
1	2	3

Total Score: _____

– If you scored 10-17, your marriage and family are way out of balance. Although you have good intentions, your priorities need a major tune up.

– If you scored 18-24, you are somewhat out of balance. As a married couple and as parents, you need to fine tune your priorities based on the principles from this chapter and throughout this book.

– If you scored 25-30, you should have written this chapter instead of me. You have a balanced family. Continue to challenge yourself to follow God's design for your marriage and family.

The Basics of Creative Priorities

• Marriage is God's top priority in the family. A great marriage is the best gift you can give your children.

• Parenting is the process of teaching and training children to leave your home, cleave to a spouse, and weave a family of their own.

• It is possible to smother our children with too much attention. The attention we give them must be balanced with the priority of marriage in the home.

• A weekly or semi-monthly "date night" will revolutionize your marriage and family.

• Schedule at least one entire night free for family time and at least 3 meals around the dinner table each week.

• Each season, evaluate the extra-curricular activities (ECAs) of your family and make sure they are not encroaching upon the top priority of your marriage or your family's connection to the local church. Try to limit each child to one ECA per season.

CHAPTER 7

CREATIVE HARMONY

RECREATING MARRIAGE AND FAMILY AFTER DIVORCE

It's amazing to realize that only about one-third of the households in our country reflect the traditional nuclear family unit. The Ozzie and Harriet, June and Ward Cleaver households are on the decline, meaning that the majority of America's families are single parent or blended families. Because of this overwhelming majority, I felt compelled to include a chapter in this book on the delicate, but very real issues of divorce, remarriage and the blended family.

Before I get into the challenges of recreating marital and family harmony after divorce, I want to go all the way back to the beginning and look at God's model for marriage. Whether you are marrying for the first time or are in the process or remarrying, you must understand that God's original intent was for one man and one woman to come together in a marriage covenant.

After we look at God's model for marriage, we will address God's concessions for divorce. People ask me all the time, "Ed, What does the Bible say about divorce? When is it biblically okay to divorce?" So, I am also going to answer those questions in this chapter. I want to assure you right up front that, if you are divorced, there is hope for you. God is a God of second chances and that includes remarriage.

Finally, after considering the biblical grounds for divorce, we will hit the home stretch by taking a look at the unique struggles of trying to start over again. How do you know when it's time to remarry? What do you need to be aware of as you consider another potential mate? How can you make a harmonious new family out of so many dissonant parts? The term "blended family" is something of a misnomer, because the blended family is anything but blended in the beginning. It is my intention to show you that there is hope for you to experience harmony and unity in your new relationship as you ground your new marriage and family in the ways of the Lord.

GOD'S MODEL FOR MARRIAGE

As we consider God's design for marriage, what better place to start than in Genesis 2:24? This whole concept is summed up in a neat little package, "For this reason a man will leave his father and mother and be united with his wife and they will become one flesh." You would think at first glance that the closest relationship on the planet would be a blood relationship, a parent-child relationship. But that is not the case, because God says in His word that something powerful and magnetic will transpire when a man loves a woman.

A man and a woman, don't miss this, are actually going to leave the close blood relationships of their father and mother, and they are going to get together in something God calls "marriage." And then, God tells us, a one-flesh relationship will occur. The Hebrew term for "one flesh" means to be melted together, to be inseparably linked. What were once two completely separate parts has become one unified component. You can't get the pieces apart.

> THE HEBREW TERM FOR "ONE FLESH" MEANS TO BE MELTED TOGETHER, TO BE INSEPARABLY LINKED.

Think about what happens when you mix together green and yellow Play Dough. No matter how you try to pull the two colors apart, the green Play Dough will always be part of the yellow, and vice versa. That is what happens when people come together in marriage. God says there will be so much trust, love, vulnerability and commitment in this one-flesh relationship that it will be the greatest human relationship in the world.

Now let's allow our minds to wander back a little bit

farther to the garden. Adam and Eve had a great marriage. Like everything else in God's creation, it was created perfect. That is, before sin entered the world. Adam and Eve were sensitive to one another and to God. They had tender hearts. When God would say, "Adam, take care of the animals," he would respond, "Yes, Lord. I love you, Lord." He was obedient and he enjoyed a special intimate relationship with his Creator. When God said, "Adam, take care of Eve" and "Eve, meet Adam's needs," they would do it. Everything was flowing perfectly in this God-designed relationship.

Something happened that destroyed this pristine environment. Adam was made as a creature in the image of God with a freedom of choice and he chose to rebel against God. He said, "God, I'm going to pave my own path. God, I am going to forge my own future. I'm going to eat this fruit off this tree. I'm not that concerned about this silly rule." The moment he did that, he exchanged his tender heart for a concrete heart. And because of Adam's sin, we have all inherited that same concrete heart and rebellious spirit. In short, we are for us and against God.

Do you remember when you dated your spouse? Think back to that time for a moment. When you dated your spouse, I'll bet you were pretty sensitive to him or her. I know that Lisa and I were very sensitive. We had these special nicknames. Lisa used to call me "Pumpkin." I called her "Princess." Our favorite song was "Get Closer" by Seals and Croft. Wow, that's a blast from the past, isn't it? When something would happen to damage the relationship, even a slight misunderstanding, we would come together very quickly, "Oh baby, I'm sorry. Did I hurt you?" You are tender-hearted, aren't you? The last thing you wanted to do is upset the proverbial apple cart. Everything was flowing, growing and going.

Then you got married, and things began to change.

Let's just consider an average American couple. For the purposes of this illustration, we will name the husband, Cal Concrete, and the wife, Kim Concrete. This average American couple decides to get married. They have a lovely ceremony and go on an incredible and romantic honeymoon. After the honeymoon the months roll by, maybe the years, and they begin to get into a pattern. An insignificant thing happens one day and they get into a little argument, a fight, but they don't really reconcile. Over time, the little arguments like these build up and the tension builds up slowly but surely. One day, it all blows up in your face. Cal and Kim have a major argument with years of unresolved baggage loading them down. Ugly and regretful things are said.

Cal and Kim Concrete have drifted apart because of the sin of unresolved conflict in their relationship. Once this crack starts to appear, the Evil One begins to widen the crack until it becomes a giant chasm. The Evil One jumps into the cab of a giant cement truck, backs the cement truck up to

Cal Concrete and deposits a load of cement into his spirit, causing him to develop a concrete heart. Cal has turned from being tender-hearted and sensitive to one hard-hearted dude. He crosses his arms defiantly and says, "If she thinks I am going to come back to her, that woman has another thing coming. I'm waiting for her to apologize for all the things she has done to mess our marriage up. I don't care what the Bible says about taking the initiative. It's her fault, so she's the one who needs to make it right!"

At the precise moment this exchange is taking place, the Evil One pulls up that cement truck and deposits a load of cement into Kim's spirit. Now she too is burdened with a concrete heart and says something very similar to what her husband said. The Evil One, though, is not the only one working. All the while that this chasm is forming between Cal and Kim Concrete, the Holy Spirit is waging his own battle. He is whispering, "Hey guys, you forgot Ephesians 4:32, 'Be kind and compassionate to one another, forgiving each other, just as in Christ God forgave you.' Let me soften your heart toward one another by giving you the power of forgiveness and reconciliation."

Cal chooses to ignore the soft voice of the Holy Spirit and, one day, he notices an attractive girl at work. He says to himself, "You know, I bet she's sensitive. She looks better than my wife, and I can tell she's sweet." An emotional attachment begins to form, and then a physical relationship develops—adultery. He is entangled in an extramarital affair. Because of a weak attempt, or no attempt at all at reconciliation, this husband becomes another statistic. And the same thing is likely to occur with Kim. She sees a man, gets emotionally attached to him, and steps down the path of adultery and divorce.

The Evil One feeds Cal and Kim many lies. "Hey, go for that relationship. You will really be satisfied over there with him! You want to be happy, don't you? Let her meet your emotional needs. He is the one you meant to be with in the first place." The Holy Spirit, though, is still there whispering, "Remember, the relationship between the husband and wife is a picture of Christ's relationship to the church. It is about commitment, and it is there for life." And on and on it goes, back and forth.

The story of this average American couple sounds familiar, doesn't it? It sounds so biting and so real, because it happens every day. You see, God knows that we don't live in a spiritual utopia. He knows we don't live in a perfect world. God is well aware of our predisposition to develop a concrete-like heart, and He knows we are going to mess up and make marital mistakes. But even in the midst of those mistakes, those hard-hearted episodes, God's model is one man, one woman together forever in marriage. He has provided the spiritual tools through the Holy Spirit to work through those marital foul-ups and experience reconciliation. We have been discussing those various tools throughout the pages of this book. Sometimes, though, the mistakes are so egregious that reconciliation seems impossible, and we feel that we are only left with one option—divorce.

GOD'S CONCESSIONS FOR DIVORCE

God proclaimed boldly in Malachi 2:16, "I hate divorce." However, Scripture has allowed some concessions for divorce. The model is one man, one woman, but I am going to share with you three biblical grounds for divorce. I give you these three grounds with caution, and only after spending countless hours in research, in discussion with theologians, pastors, leaders, and scholars over my twenty years of ministry. I must caution you not to look at these three grounds as a way out, an escape clause of the marital covenant. There is no fine print in this marital covenant. "Oh boy, I finally have a reason to ditch this person."

God says, first and foremost, that you need to look for a way through instead of a way out. So many people today are ready to throw commitment out like a sack

> I MUST CAUTION YOU NOT TO LOOK AT THESE THREE GROUNDS AS A WAY OUT, AN ESCAPE CLAUSE OF THE MARITAL COVENANT. THERE IS NO FINE PRINT IN THIS MARITAL COVENANT.

of trash. They throw away trust and they throw away love, asking themselves, "What's in it for me," as they jump from one relationship to the next.

However, when Christian counseling has been used, when prayer and hard work have been exhausted, God has granted three grounds for biblical divorce and remarriage, so let's take a look at those. God's first concession is found in 2 Corinthians 5:17. This passage, I believe, indicates that we are free to remarry when a divorce has occurred prior to establishing a personal relationship with Jesus Christ. God tells us, "Therefore, if anyone is in Christ, he is a new creation (with the exception of divorce)." Is that what it says? No. He says, "Therefore, if anyone is in Christ, he is a new creation; the old is gone (that means divorce, that means peddling drugs, that means illicit behavior, that means any sin we could possibly think of), the new has come."

The word "new" here in the original language means new in form and quality. So, if I have divorced prior to my salvation, prior to my personal relationship with Jesus Christ, the Bible says I am free to marry again, to make a fresh start as a new person in Christ—as long as the new marriage is to another believer (2 Cor. 6:14).

The second concession He makes, (found in Matthew 19:9) is sexual immorality or marital unfaithfulness. Christ is speaking specifically about adultery (which also includes homosexual conduct) in this passage.

The men of Jesus' day were divorcing their wives for ridiculous reasons, like her hair was too long, she had morning breath, she was overweight, and so on. They were getting divorces, left and right, for illegitimate reasons. Jesus cuts to the quick, "I tell you that anyone who divorces his wife except for marital unfaithfulness, and marries another woman, commits adultery."

I do not believe Jesus is saying, nor is He implying, that a one-night stand is automatically a cause for divorce. The Bible certainly does not condone this kind of behavior, but I know many, many marriages that have survived a onetime affair and are flourishing today by the grace and mercy of God. If there is a pattern of unfaithfulness, it is one of the biblical grounds for divorce.

The third concession God gives us is in the case of desertion by an unbeliever. We find the scriptural support for this concession in 1 Corinthians 7:15, "But if the unbeliever leaves, let him do so." A believing man or woman is not bound to their unbelieving spouse in such circumstances. God has called us to live in peace. If a believer is married to an unbeliever, he or she is to live out their faith in a quiet, reverent and holy manner. But if the unbeliever deserts the believer, the believer is free to remarry.

I believe a good argument can also be made that this particular concession applies to situations of sexual or physical abuse against a spouse or children. In a sense, the abusing spouse (whether a professing Christian or not) has spiritually deserted their family by endangering them with a pattern of deviant behavior that is both illegal and immoral. I would even question whether such a person could truly be a believer in Christ, if they indeed profess to be one. While abuse, or other ongoing criminal activity is not given as an explicit reason for divorce, it seems to be implicit within this broader concession of desertion.

NOW WHAT?

One night, a close friend of comedian and satirist, W.C. Fields, walked into his dressing room to find W.C. reading the Bible. Now, you have to understand something about W.C. Fields if you are not familiar with him. He was known to be a wild man; a womanizer, a drunk, and a poison-tongued performer. In short, he was immoral. Here, though, was W.C. propped back in his chair in front of the make-up mirror reading the Bible. As he saw Fields thumbing through the pages of Scripture, this friend was shocked. He said, "W.C., what has happened? Why are you, of all people, reading the Bible?" W.C. Field's responded in classic style in that one-of-a-kind voice, "I'm just looking for loopholes. Looking for loopholes."

Too many of us read the Bible and we look for loopholes. "Oh, there is a way out. Great, I can divorce her, I can divorce him, and go along the primrose path." There is no primrose path after divorce. Believe me, I've seen many shattered marriages and the path leading from those broken relationships is always a rocky and difficult one. God always wants us to look for a way to work through the problem. He does not give us these concessions for divorce as an easy out, but as a last resort.

The fact is, though, many have made the decision to divorce for one reason or another. You may be one of those people. And the question on your mind is, "Now what? Where do I go from here?" Let me encourage you that divorce is not the unpardonable sin. God can make something new and wonderful out of the pieces of a broken marriage and family. You can still achieve God's ideal for marriage the second time around.

> DIVORCE IS NOT THE UNPARDONABLE SIN. GOD CAN MAKE SOMETHING NEW AND WONDERFUL OUT OF THE PIECES OF A BROKEN MARRIAGE AND FAMILY.

So, with that in mind, I want to spend the remainder of this chapter outlining some creative ways to achieve a harmonious mix in a "blended family." Starting over after divorce is usually not just about you and your new spouse, because children are often involved. We will address remarriage, therefore, from the perspective of both the adults and children involved in this new blended family situation.

CREATING A CREATIVE FAMILY BLEND

I want to share with you how you can have harmony in your new family. I want to share with you how you can experience unity and harmony in this recreated family band. To do this, I will use musical metaphors to illustrate the harmony you can achieve in a blended family. Paul encourages in Philippines 4:2, "Live in harmony in the Lord." This applies to single adults. It applies to those who are married within a nuclear family. It also applies to the single parent family and the blended family. We are to live in harmony in the Lord.

In other words, God loves you and me so much that He cannot stand the thought of His people experiencing dissonance in their lives as a result of sin. His desire is for us to live in harmony with Him. He doesn't promise us an easy life by any means, but He does promise to be our God who will protect and loves us unconditionally. "Well, how do I get that, Ed? I am remarried in a blended family. I am a single parent and dealing with all of this mess. How do I experience harmony?"

AUDITION THE PLAYERS

Let's start with the basics, because the first thing you have to do, if you are considering remarriage and doing the blended family gig, is to audition the prospective musicians. If you talk to any good music director, he spends a good amount of time doing something called audition work. If a director or conductor just picked people at random to be a part of a band or choir, he would end up in chaos. The audience would say, "Oh, they have the worst music in the world. It doesn't make sense. It sounds like everyone is just doing his or her own thing. There's no mixing or blending."

It takes time to audition, to interview, and to determine how the individual parts of the band come together. If you are considering remarriage, if you are considering taking on the blended family gig, you had better take time to interview all the prospective band members prior to marriage. Sit down with them, get to know them, and see how they mesh; because that's the time to discover how they will come together. Don't wait until after you are married to audition the prospective players.

Research and experience tell us that it takes two years emotionally to get over the death of a spouse or the trauma of divorce. So make sure you date your future mate long enough for everyone involved, the man, the woman and the children, to get to a point where they are able to act naturally around each other.

We can all fool people; we are pros at doing that. We put on that game-show-host smile, so others will think that we never have a bad day. We work hard at giving the impression that everything is always perfect and that we are ready to tackle the world. All the while, though, we are hiding our true emotions inside. It takes time to see others for whom they truly are, so give everyone involved the time they need to feel comfortable enough around each other so that they are able to behave naturally. You need time to discern why your divorce took place, and, if appropriate, why your future wife got her divorce. You need time to heal yourself spiritually and recalibrate anything in your life that is impeding your relationship with Christ. Can you handle the fact that his kids will potentially have two Dads? Will all the complex relationships mesh together?

We serve a God of second, third and fourth chances. His grace keeps going and going and going. Just because you have been divorced, it is not the end of the world. You don't have to fly coach spiritually speaking, as if you have to hide behind the curtain for the rest of your life, just because you have been divorced. Yes, you can still fly first class. God might lead you into the blended family unit, into a remarriage situation, just so you can have a second chance to achieve God's ideal. You must take time to get to know and understand the dynamics of everyone involved before taking the leap into a blended family situation.

REHEARSE, DON'T REPEAT

Musicians rehearse over and over again to keep from repeating past mistakes and to engrain positive patterns for the future. Hopefully and prayerfully, you come to the marital table during a second marriage with more maturity and with the experience of learning from past mistakes.

Something I have seen, though, over the years in talking with and counseling so many young people is that those who come from divorced homes lean toward getting divorced in their own lives. If you have parents who have been divorced, you are more likely to get a divorce. And I have to ask, why in the world is that a trend? Why is that happening in such overwhelming numbers?

Here is one major reason why I believe this trend exists. Parents who get a divorce are not teaching their children to learn from their mistakes. If you are in this situation, take time, energy, and effort to rehearse with your children where you went wrong and what you should have done differently. Take them aside and say, "This is where Daddy messed up. This is where Mommy messed up. Divorce is not the best way to do it. I was wrong in this area, and this is what I should have done and what you should do in a relationship." Learn from your mistakes, and help your children learn from them as well. After explaining where you went wrong, begin modeling the godly way to structure a family. A family that is centered upon God and His word.

FOCUS ON THE RIGHT SCORE

Also, if you are thinking about remarriage into a blended

family, take your eyes off the musical score of the nuclear family and focus on this new blended family score. Stop comparing your situation to the nuclear family of one man and one woman, together forever, with 2.3 kids. That is not the blended family. The blended family is a whole different scene, with multiple family situations happening at the same time. And if you're not careful, it has the potential to be a breeding ground for jealousy, envy, complications, mistakes, and hurt feelings.

IF YOU ARE THINKING ABOUT REMARRIAGE INTO A BLENDED FAMILY, TAKE YOUR EYES OFF THE MUSICAL SCORE OF THE NUCLEAR FAMILY AND FOCUS ON THIS NEW BLENDED FAMILY SCORE.

You can be obedient to Philippians 4:2, living "in harmony in the Lord," even in the blended family. But you are going to have to spend more time in the studio, more time working, and more time listening. If Pavarotti, Mick Jagger and Garth Brooks stepped into a recording studio together, do you think they would achieve unity and harmony immediately? If they really worked at it, harmony could come. But it doesn't just happen naturally. It takes time.

When I think about dissonant family situations in the Bible, I think about Jacob in Genesis 35. Jacob had four wives (two were sisters), twelve sons, and a meddling father-in-law. They all lived together in adjoining tents. Do you think they had a few problems? You bet they did. But God brought out of that confusing family situation the twelve tribes of Israel (through Jacob's sons).

You don't have to go to movies or watch soap operas to see exciting stuff. Just read the Bible. Intrigue, espionage, murder, jealousy, envy and strife—it's all in there. And the great thing is that we can learn from the mistakes of biblical characters, so we don't have to make them ourselves. That is one of the reasons I love the Bible. God doesn't try to cover up the mistakes of His people or rationalize them away. He just lays it all on the line, so we can benefit from the shortcomings and failures of other people of faith.

Eli is a character in the book of 1 Samuel who also dealt with problems related to family harmony. Eli's two sons, Hophni and Phinehas, were out of control. Eli was a priest and his sons were stereotypical preacher's kids. I mean, these kids were over the edge. First Samuel 3:13 reveals that Eli failed in disciplining his own sons, "His sons made themselves contemptible, and he failed to restrain them." But God gave Eli a second chance by giving him Samuel to raise.

Samuel was the son of Hannah and Elkanah, who left him in Eli's charge to be brought up in the Temple as a man of God. It is evident that Eli did a much better job when he had a second chance. Samuel turned out to be one of Israel's greatest judges and prophets. Eli turned his past mistakes into future successes by learning from his failure and doing it God's way the second time around. You can too win the second time around if you keep your eyes on what God has called you to do. Stop focusing on the nuclear family, or others expectations for your life. Trust God to build a family that fears God, and is a place where His love is found through every relationship in your family.

BE SENSITIVE TO STYLE

Once you hear, "I now pronounce you husband and wife" and you are involved in the blended family, there is something else you don't want to miss. Be sensitive to the fact that each of the musicians has a different style. I am referring specifically now to the children in the blended family—the style of the child.

You might not believe this, but remarriage is more difficult and taxing on children than divorce. They are going to go through more trauma during remarriage than during the divorce. "Why?" you ask. "That doesn't make sense." Remarriage is more difficult, because, when you get remarried, it ends the thought in the child's mind that reconciliation is still possible for their mom and dad. Also, they have to accept the new family unit, with a new authority structure.

Another major issue for children, especially teenagers, is the invasion of their space. Suddenly, they have to share their stuff, maybe even their room, with new "family members" who might as well be strangers. Some of that discomfort can be alleviated by allowing sufficient time for both spouses and children to adjust to the new family prior to establishing a combined household. But it is still going to be a major adjustment.

Remember that within every family, especially the blended family, everyone needs their own stuff. If I were speaking, I would be screaming now. You need to be sure to give children their own territory, because from the child's perspective, suddenly these aliens have come in, invaded their already defined territory and are messing with their stuff. Mom and Dad, make sure every person has some space, even if it is a little corner, just for them and their personal things.

The number one reason that the divorce rate is higher the second time around is the unique child rearing challenges of the blended family. So I encourage you to take your children and your new spouse's children and audition them for the express purpose of getting to know them and becoming sensitive to their styles. If you will do this ahead of time, you will help them mesh more successfully into the new family system.

It is tempting to get so involved in the newly established marriage relationship that you tune out the changing needs of the children involved. Don't let that happen. Take the necessary time to understand and be sensitive to each child's

TAKE THE NECESSARY TIME TO UNDERSTAND AND BE SENSITIVE TO EACH CHILD'S UNIQUE STYLE, BEFORE AND AFTER THE NEW MARRIAGE BEGINS.

unique style, before and after the new marriage begins.

Recently, I pulled up to a busy intersection in the Dallas-Fort Worth area and I heard, and felt, rap music coming from the car behind me. I glanced back and saw this guy singing along like nobody's business to this rap song. People around him in the other cars were looking at him and laughing. The guy, though, was totally oblivious. He was so into his style, it was like the rest of the world was not even there.

I see parents in a blended family doing the same thing. They have this love that is so fresh, so dynamic, and so all-encompassing with their new spouse, that these two love birds forget about how it is affecting the kids involved on both sides. Meanwhile, the kids are thinking, "This blended family thing is the worst." The new family is not just about Mom (or step-mom) and Dad (or step-dad). This is an all-for-one and one-for-all deal. It's about everyone involved. Are you sensitive to the styles of your children?

THROW OUT THE 8-TRACKS

If you are going to have this harmony and unity, and not dissonance, learn how to sing a new song. In Psalms 33:3, David writes, "Sing to him a new song." I am sure the first time David pulled out the harp and started strumming a new song, people probably said, "Oh my, he is not singing traditional hymns any more; the guy has gone contemporary. Who is this long-haired shepherd boy singing these rock songs? What has gotten into these Hebrew kids?" Well, David was singing a new song. Just like David, the blended family has to learn to sing a new song.

Do you know what tears blended families apart? Do you know what tears apart single parent families? It is the 8-track tape mentality. Do you remember leisure suits and 8-track tapes? Be honest. I must confess that I had a lime green leisure suit, and it didn't have lapels—a serious fashion emergency. I thought this leisure suit, unlike some that had giant lapels that looked like elephant ears, was the greatest thing in the world. I also had an 8-track tape player, and my favorite tape was "The Best of the Bee Gees." Talk about retro.

So many make the mistake, in the blended family and single parent family, of going retro with an 8-track tape mentality. What am I talking about? I am taking about not letting go of the anger and resentment of the broken relationship, "Oh, my spouse, my ex, is such a jerk." These folks play the tape of bitterness over and over and over again. They replay it for their ex-spouse, their new spouse, and then they let the kids hear it a few hundred times. The bitterness escalates and spreads like a disease. As they continue to attack their ex, he or she returns the favor by attacking back.

How do you break out of the 8-track tape mentality? Take the 8-track tape out, throw it away, and put in a CD. For this purpose, CD stands for something different: Christian

Deliverance. And what specifically is playing on this CD? Philippians 3:13-14, "Brothers, I do not consider myself yet to have taken hold of it. But one thing I do: Forgetting what is behind and straining toward what is ahead, I press on toward the goal to win the prize for which God has called me heavenward in Christ Jesus."

What a powerful verse! This is one of my life verses. In fact, I preached from this passage the first Sunday I ever spoke at Fellowship Church. The Apostle Paul was advising his friends at Philippi to forget the past and move forward. Anything in the past that keeps you from progress, you had better forget it.

I am glad we serve a God who tells me and tells you to forget what lies behind. Instead He says, "Reach forward to what lies ahead." Isn't that great? You can't forget, you can't reach forward, you can't press on, if you look into the past and are wearing out those 8-track tapes. It is time to put in that CD of Christian Deliverance and sing a new song. Confess your sins, deal with them, work through the grief, and then move out ahead. God has a new agenda, a new course, a new avenue, a new highway for the blended family. God can give you the power to put the past behind you and press on.

CREATE HARMONY

I'm not a great singer, but I had the opportunity to be involved in a musical performance many years ago at my father's church in Houston, Texas. The music director of this church walked up to me one day and said, "Ed, I'm doing a musical and putting together a barbershop quartet and, since you have a really low voice, I wondered if you would like singing the bass part? Would you consider it, Ed?"

I replied, "Well, no, I have never done that before. I don't know the first thing about singing in a barbershop quartet." He kept after me until finally I relented, "Okay, I will try out for it. I'll do the audition."

This is what my audition consisted of. He said, "Okay, Ed, find the lowest note that you can possibly produce and hold it there for about ten seconds." I did exactly that. I sang, or rumbled, the lowest note I could and held it for several seconds. And then he said, "That's it, Ed. You've got it." I said "What?" He said, "That's it, that's all we need." So the day of the big event came at the Music Hall in downtown Houston, and I was the bass singer in the barbershop quartet. When he nodded to me, I would just let out that one note until he cut me off. People came up to me afterwards and said, "Oh, what a beautiful voice. That was unbelievable. You sure know how to create that harmony, Ed."

I couldn't help but laugh at their applause and compliments, because I knew how pathetic I sounded without the talent of the three other men and the guidance of the music director. Creating that kind of harmony was definitely a group effort. And that is what we are talking about with the blended family: Creating harmony together. How do you harmonize as a family? Too many of us are relationally tone deaf, or we are operating without musical direction, and we don't know how to harmonize with each other.

In seminary I was required to take a music class where I learned the basics of conducting. If you are really going to do the blended family gig, you have to establish harmony in the home by becoming co-conductors with your spouse. You need to join hands with your spouse and learn how to conduct your blended family together. If you don't, Mom will be reading one piece of music and Dad will be reading another piece of music. And that's how you spell dissonance. You have to come together, have one musical sheet in front of you as your guide.

When you direct, though, make sure that you don't try to improvise and defect from the sheet of music from which you have both agreed to conduct. That is an easy temptation to fall into in the blended family. What often happens is that initially you agree with your spouse to become co-conductors in discipline, in responsibilities, and in rules. Then, as time goes by and the rubber hits the road, you begin to cut a little more slack with your biological children than with your stepchildren. You begin to get a little more sensitive and defensive about their needs, and you start to defect from the musical piece you've all agreed to play.

It is human nature to be more protective of your own

biological children and to want to have more freedom with them. Make sure, though, that you sit down with your spouse and set forth in writing what every person's responsibility will be in the blended family. Also, define how those various responsibilities will mesh with or bleed over into the ex-spouse's family unit. You must set those principles, put them down and direct together.

This includes working with your ex-spouse in the other household and having some common ground on which you can both stand for the sake of the children. The children must feel, especially in a joint-custody situation, that they are vital members of both households. This can only happen when everyone works together from the same page to make it happen.

SINGLE PARENTS

I want to push the pause button and address a specific issue facing single parents that can spill over into the blended family when they choose to remarry. We have so many single parents in society today, and I think they have one of the most difficult and underappreciated roles in our society. I have seen so many wonderful things happen over the years as God has worked through and touched single parents, giving them power and ability well beyond their years and capacity. I want to share with you several things you need to understand in regard to this single parent game.

When a divorce occurs, the wife usually experiences a significant cut in personal income. Because the wife is the custodial parent in ninety percent of the cases, her earning potential goes down as she attempts to juggle her work responsibilities with the increased demands of single parenting. The man, on the other hand, experiences a substantial increase in his personal income, because he is now able to devote most of his time to work.

Single moms, throughout this whole scenario, are especially susceptible to feelings of guilt. They feel guilty for putting your children through the divorce, for being spread too thin between the home and career fronts, and for not being able to do more for their kids financially. Single moms, you can feel so guilty and so bitter that you end up trying to get rid of the guilt by becoming overly permissive with your children. Watch out for this tendency. You will allow your children to do anything, because you reason, "Well, if I am a nice Mom, then I can make up for these other problems caused by my divorce." Your children suddenly begin to run over you, and you treat them like one of your peers. And the authority base is gone.

Let's briefly shift gears to single dads. You feel guilty, single dad, because you are not as involved with your kids on a day-to-day basis like your ex-wife. And your guilt leads you to become the purchasing parent. You've got the extra cash, so on weekend visits, the entertainment, excitement, and the adventure is all happening with dad. You ease the guilt by getting into this sugar daddy mentality. Again, the authority base disappears and your kids tumble into a free fall of deteriorating structure and discipline.

A single mom and her three children live just a few houses down from ours, and even a casual observer on this street will notice a recurring event in that household. Once a week, this woman's ex-husband will turn down the street in his black SUV, pull up to the house and walk to the door. A few minutes later, he will come out with the kids and will proceed to take them to his home for the weekend. One week—this is the quintessential single dad—as he turned the corner, I noticed that in the back of his truck he had brought with him an enormous box from Toys R Us. He drove up to the house as usual, walked to the door and out came his excited children, "Oh, Daddy's got a new toy! See you, Mom."

Single parents, I am talking to both moms and dads right now. Please make sure you deal with the guilt between you and God and between you and your ex-spouse so that the effects of that guilt don't spill out onto your children. If you are going to mess up, mess up on the side of being too strict, rather than having a permissive mentality that says, "Well, kids, if it feels good do it. You can do whatever you want and have whatever you want. I just want to make you happy."

THE BLENDED FAMILY

Let's release the pause button now and fast forward to the blended family. What often happens, when single mom or single dad remarries and enters a blended family situation, is that this permissive parenting style continues. That is why (in many circumstances) children run the show in the blended family. They ran the show when mom and dad were single, so they think the same rules apply in the blended family and they can run the show again. Only this time, the stakes are even higher. You have to establish that authority before you remarry so you can maintain that authority as co-directors in the blended family. Talk to any member of a band or orchestra and they will tell you that someone has to call the shots. Mom and Dad must present a unified front as co-conductors.

Another aspect to being a good director and establishing harmony in the home is respecting the routines of the new family system. Establish your own routines as a blended family, but also respect the routines of the other family, especially during the holiday shuffle. As the kids fly from destination-to-destination, be extra sensitive to both your children's needs and those of the other family involved. Also, step up to the relational plate and do as much as you can to enhance your child's relationship with your ex-spouse.

If you have a problem with the ex-spouse, don't tell

your child: "Well your Dad's just a jerk. That's why we got a divorce." If you have a problem with him, if he is truly being a jerk, talk to him about it. Don't use your child as a go-between or as relational ammunition. By being a parent and role model, even in the midst of your toughest relational challenges, you can give your children the tools they need to establish lasting relationships later in life.

We have addressed several key issues related to divorce and remarriage in this chapter. We have looked at God's ideal for marriage and also some biblical concessions for divorce. Following that, we discussed the opportunity for a second chance to achieve that marital ideal in the blended family. As you follow the principles related to creating a creative family blend—auditioning the players, rehearsing not repeating, focusing on the right score, being sensitive to style, replacing your 8-tracks with CDs, and becoming co-conductors—you can experience the harmony of everyone pulling together in this new family band. And that is the kind of music God loves to hear.

The Basics of Creative Harmony

• Remember that God's model is one man and one woman together in marriage and that He has provided the resources (through the Holy Spirit) to carry you through rocky times.

• Receive the reconciliation of God's grace and power so you can overcome the obstacles from divorce. God does hate divorce, but He can reconcile all things to give you another opportunity to do marriage His way.

• Take time to heal after a divorce (2-3 years) before you decide to remarry.

• Let God heal you so you can focus on the future rather than the past.

• Single parents should maintain control of their children despite the pressures to treat their children as if they were peers.

CHAPTER 8

MARITAL FAQS

ANSWERS TO SOME FREQUENTLY ASKED
QUESTIONS ABOUT MARRIAGE

Over the last several chapters we have addressed issues like the Marital Work Ethic, creative communication, conflict resolution and the popular, yet often avoided subject of sex with a chapter on sex builders and busters. We also addressed the very important subject of money and marriage and the challenge of keeping your family spouse-centric rather than kid-centric. And finally, in the previous chapter, we tackled the difficult issues of divorce and remarriage.

In this chapter, Lisa and I will answer some frequently asked questions (FAQs) regarding marriage. These questions were solicited from people at our church during a series on marriage and represent, we believe, problems and issues for nearly ever marital relationship.

Before we take a look at these questions, let me say

something that you need to understand. Lisa and I are not experts on marriage. We do enjoy a great marriage, and the reason we do is because we have built our lives on the principles found in God's word. We have done this individually, and we have done it together as a couple.

I know some who will read this book are single adults. The church is full of single adults who are planning for, dreaming of, and thinking about marriage. On any given Sunday, about forty-five to fifty percent of those who attend Fellowship Church are single. We want to address some of the questions that singles have about marriage.

All married couples experience varying degrees of difficulty at different times in their marriage. We will do our best to address some of the issues you are dealing with right now in this final chapter.

It is a pipe dream for Lisa and me to think that we can understand and feel exactly what you are feeling. We can, on the other hand, hit on these common marital issues, and direct you to the material and counselors out there who can help make your marriage a creative and lasting marriage.

Q: The first chapter talked about the value of the marriage vows. If I have already said these vows, or will in the future, how do I know for sure the other person is the right one?

ED: Well, hopefully you know that your fiancée is the right one prior to standing before a pastor, God, and some friends for the event! What I share with singles in counseling situations comes from both the Bible and from life experiences. I have written a book, entitled "The Ulti-Mate: Finding the Love of Your Life," which breaks down a lot of what I teach. But let me give you the Cliff's Notes of this book. If you are single and are considering a specific someone as a possible life partner, I think there are several tests that you need to take him or her through.

The first test would be the spiritual test. You need to make sure that they know Christ personally. I am not talking about just lip service, but an actual story about their life before Christ, what happened when they met the Lord and what God has done since that important event.

When you are both operating from the same spiritual dynamic, it forms the foundation for conflict resolution. Marriage is about conflict in a real way. You have two self-centered sinners trying to do life God's way, so you need to be on the same page spiritually and also have knowledge of the ministry of reconciliation.

We need to try to understand the idea that God sent Christ to die on the cross for our sins, something

WHEN YOU ARE BOTH OPERATING FROM THE SAME SPIRITUAL DYNAMIC, IT FORMS THE FOUNDATION FOR CONFLICT RESOLUTION.

that we don't deserve, and that He rose again. If we have accepted that, we have been given the ability and motivation to want to make our issues right before God and before our spouse.

Speaking of the spiritual test, it also helps in raising children. Lisa and I have four children. Child rearing is challenging, and I don't know where we would be without that common bond of Christ.

I would also use the character test. It is important to measure the other person's character. Because Lisa and I dated for a long time, I was able to observe her in various situations. Honesty, responsibility, endurance and other important qualities like these can only be seen over the long haul.

Another test would be the one of just kicking back, hanging out, and living life on the rugged plains of reality. You might call this the time test. If you are dating and contemplating marriage, I would advise dating at least 12 months. What this does is it allows infatuation to fade like a good pair of jeans. It will help you discern the relationship through good times and bad. Time will also allow you to expose the relationship to family and friends. We all know there's nothing quite as helpful as the counsel we receive from the people that know us best.

———

Q: Lisa, when did you know that Ed was the right one for you?

LISA: As Ed mentioned, we dated for six years. We met when we had just finished our freshman year of high school. We had dated just one year when Ed told me that we were going to get married. I told him that was great, but I wanted to grow up and be a flight attendant and fly all over the world. I told him he would have to wait until after that if he really wanted to get married.

By the time we were sophomores in college, I reminded him that he had once said we were going to get married. I told him I no longer had the desire to be a flight attendant and that we should get the show on the road.

During these six years, we had already answered those questions and passed those tests. I just knew in my heart that there would be a part of me that would be empty without him. And I believed that he felt the same say.

———

Q: The third chapter addressed the importance of communication between a husband and a wife. Ed, you are the pastor of a very large church and are very, very busy. Lisa, you serve at the church as well as take care of your husband and four children. How in the world do you two build time into your marriage for communication?

LISA: We are very busy, and I think most people these days are very busy. This is definitely one of the killers of good communication. I think these days, many of us have forgotten the art of saying "no." We need to learn to let go of the good things in order to receive the best things in life.

Ed and I are very intentional about building time together on a daily and weekly basis in order to communicate. It doesn't just happen. There will always be a child that needs us. There will always be people in our church who need us. So we are very intentional about it.

We try to structure time on a daily basis after the children are in bed for the night. I am a very structured person, and we are big on enforcing an established bedtime during school nights. We also have a high-school-aged daughter who goes to bed later than our younger children, but she is upstairs having her quiet time in the evenings so we can enjoy some adult time together. Another important element is what we do with our extra-curricular activities (ECAs). We say no to a lot of these ECAs that can get in the way of our time together in the evenings.

Also, we do not have a television in our bedroom. A great thing happened when the TV in our bedroom broke. This "TV-free zone" has created a better atmosphere for communication. If you have a TV in your bedroom, be very friendly with the OFF button. That time together in silence will allow you to communicate. This communication can lead you to some great "other things" as well. Enough said.

And then there is our date night, which Ed has already addressed earlier in the book. We schedule one at least every other week, but we try to date every week. If the daily communication has been difficult, by Thursday night we know we will be together for an uninterrupted time.

Oftentimes on our dates, I have the calendar in hand so that we can go over our schedule for the next week. Humorous maybe, but that may be the only time we have to actually schedule things we want to do. If we don't schedule well in advance, time will be eaten away by other things.

ED: We have to fight for that time. I would say that in the fifteen years since we have been in Dallas, it has been the date night that has taken our marriage to the next level. You know, it's great to go out with other couples, but that concentrated time for just the two of us is crucial.

LISA: On occasion we go out with others, but we keep it balanced. There have been times when I have had meetings at the school and have had to excuse myself for not attending. I used to wish I had some big excuse other than the fact that Ed and I were going on a date that night. But I finally got the courage to say that, and the other wives were falling all over themselves to tell me how great that was. This concept became something that many of my friends wanted to adopt for themselves.

————

Q: What do you think is the most important thing that a spouse can communicate to his or her partner?

ED: I would say that self-esteem is right up there. Both the husband and the wife get much of their self-esteem and value from each other. Oftentimes, I have forgotten the importance of my words to Lisa. Maybe I have said a word of criticism to Lisa. Maybe Lisa has done something really incredible, and I have not really complemented her the way I should have. I am trying to improve my sensitivity in this area because I haven't been as consistent as I should be.

I think of our church. I have the opportunity to speak before a lot of people several times per weekend. I certainly enjoy it when people come up to tell me they like the message or the church. That means a lot. But there is nothing like having Lisa turn to me on the way home and say, "Honey, I really appreciated that message. It really blessed my heart." There is nothing like hearing that from my spouse. The self-esteem thing is big. Don't forget the little things either. Things like honoring her with positive body language and big hugs are also very meaningful.

LISA: I feel it is important for Ed to show me that I am valuable, and for me to show him that he is valuable. We do that by being intentional about our communication, and having that time alone together.

We also have to be careful about the things that we do which could possibly devalue our spouse, like mentioning them in a negative light in public conversation, setting up a date night and not showing up, or spending time on the cell phone instead of being alone with them. You also have to be careful in how you convey messages to your spouse through both tone of voice and words. When Ed and I speak words of value to each other, we gain more confidence in one another, and gain confidence in our marriage.

———

Q: Moving from communication to conflict resolution, how do you two handle financial stress in your marriage?

ED: Many couples have financial stress and pressure. Maybe one of the spouses is a drive-by spender and the other one is more conservative. This is often the case in marriage. Or maybe both are drowning in the seas of debt. There is no pressure like financial pressure on the marriage relationship.

I challenge husbands and wives to have a biblical view of money. What Lisa and I have tried to do over the years of our marriage is acknowledge that everything that we have comes from God. That is a no-brainer for us.

Usually we sit down at the beginning of the year and go over our budget for the coming twelve months. We live pretty much by the ten-ten-eighty principle. We give at least ten percent to the church. We have given much more than that at times, but that is our baseline. Then we try to save at least ten percent. We live on the remaining eighty percent. When we are talking and praying about the budget, these give us some basic guidelines.

I think that some couples make serious mistakes when one spouse has an account that the other doesn't know about, a little 007-style action. I think that there should be full disclosure, and that you need to talk about major purchases together.

> WITH THE REMAINING EIGHTY PERCENT, AFTER GIVING AND SAVING, IT IS ABOUT HOW WE CAN USE WISELY WHAT GOD HAS BLESSED US WITH TO PAY OUR BILLS, TO EAT AND TO ENJOY OURSELVES.

LISA: Usually, we talk about the goals we have for the year. I like to talk about furniture and Ed usually likes to discuss his next fishing trip. We talk about our family vacation and we put in money for emergencies. We don't go into that conversation selfishly, but think about one another and the whole family picture. With the remaining eighty percent, after giving and saving, it is about how we can use wisely what God has blessed us with to pay our bills, to eat and to enjoy ourselves.

Q: *You talked about full disclosure regarding finances. What is your view on pre-nuptial agreements that people use to negotiate a marriage?*

ED: If someone is thinking about a pre-nuptial agreement, I would challenge them to seriously consider the reasons why they feel it is needed. Are they unsure of the other person? Is there an element of distrust or uncertainty about that person or about whether the marriage will last? If that's the case, they need to rethink the marriage or begin some pre-marital counseling to work through those issues. Generally speaking, I don't like these types of agreements in marriage because I don't think that you should go into marriage with a question mark. You should go into marriage with an exclamation point.

LISA: Now, understand that we had less than $1,800 to our name when we got married.

ED: Well, that's true! Even so, that is still what I'd advise. You don't want to go into marriage being unsure. Trust is foundational to any great marriage.

Q: *How do you deal with the controversial concept of submission in your family?*

ED: That whole issue in the Bible has been misconstrued and taken out of context. Here is what the Bible says. It says that the husband has the spiritual responsibility of the relationship. He is the leader. It doesn't mean that he is on a pedestal and the wife is below him.

We play on a level playing field before God. However, according to the Bible, the husband is to love his bride like Jesus loved the church. How much did He love the church? He laid down His life for the church. Christ took the initiative and never stops working for the church. Even though we don't deserve to be loved, He loved us.

If I love Lisa with a self-sacrificing love, she is free and will experience great freedom to be submissive. She is able to love me, yet live her life like she wants it to be done.

There are many times when we have big decisions. I think that maybe we should go a certain way, but she will point out other factors that she thinks should be included in the decision. She can, and often does bring up things that cause me to change my mind. But I know at the end of the day, as far as God's chain of command, the final decision rests on the shoulders of the husband.

LISA: I have never had a problem with the term "submission." I have had a problem submitting! When I think of this issue, I can't help think of something that happened early in our marriage.

We wanted to go visit my family in South Carolina for

Thanksgiving, but we only had a short amount of time. Both of us were in school and he was also working. Ed wanted to fly and I told him that we could not afford it, that we would have to drive. We went back and forth on this issue.

We had just gotten our first credit card, which came with a $350 limit. The tickets were going to be $175 each. I told Ed that if we bought them, we would be making a mistake. We didn't need to have debt, and I thought that we should drive instead. (Now, I did not mention that there was a piece of furniture I wanted to bring back with us) I only used the financial consequences to influence Ed's thinking.

One night, in the middle of the night, Ed sat up in bed and announced, "We are flying." He got out of bed and proceeded to make the flight arrangements in the middle of the night. I was really upset. And I must confess that on this particular occasion, I did not follow the biblical principle of resolving my anger before I went to bed.

The next day I was still fuming. Even though I was submitting on the outside, I was still very upset about it on the inside. When we got to the airport, the flight was overbooked. The gentleman at the counter said that we could have free seats on a later flight if we would give up our tickets. He also gave us money for a cab, movies and dinner.

When we eventually flew to South Carolina, we made the entire trip without spending a dime. God taught me that submission is a really good thing to practice! I realize this may be kind of an extreme example, and I'm not promising that you'll fly free if you submit to your husband. But I believe God was teaching me an important lesson about having a submissive attitude through that experience.

ED: It is interesting that the word husband in Latin is made up of two words – house and band. We are to be the band that keeps the marriage and the household together.

Let's say that in a particular situation she is 99.9% wrong and you are 0.1% wrong. Even then, husbands are to be the ones to initiate the reconciliation. That is the spiritual responsibility of the husband. Even on the days when she may be hard to love, you are to love your wife like Christ loved the church. And believe me; if you are doing that, the other pieces will take care of themselves.

LISA: It is also something that brings order to a household. Ed mentioned the chain of command. There are times when I will share with him my opinions; sometimes he takes them, other times he goes with his initial decision. He is not always right, but it is nothing that is beyond repair. We both use each decision and each circumstance as a learning lesson and recognize that this process of submission and self-sacrificing love is the order of our household.

ED: There are many other areas that Lisa leads out for our family. For example, we were talking about finances. She is the one who pays the bills. In our relationship, she is the one who happens to have a better gift in this area.

Q: How do you deal with the issue of in-laws in the marriage?

LISA: I do not have the typical mother-in-law situation. Ed and I dated for six years. There are three boys in his family and I was the only girl on the scene for a very long time. And to be honest with you, Ed's mother spoiled me rotten. She and I had a great relationship from the very beginning, and we still have a great relationship today. When she comes to visit, it's a lot of fun for me to have her here.

However, in the early days of our marriage, my family lived in South Carolina and we lived in Houston, very close to Ed's family. I had done that leave and cleave part that the Bible talks about in Genesis 2. I left my family and I was holding very tightly to the relationship I had with my new husband.

Ed, on the other hand, was still very close to his family. He continued to do things just about the same way he had always done things. If I expected him home for dinner, he might be over there shooting baskets with his brothers. When I would find him, I would ask what he was doing, and he would say that he was home—but not our home! So, it was kind of tough in those early days.

ED: I think I had a tougher time cutting the cord than she did. Also, living in Houston and working at the same church where my father was (and still is) the pastor was great, but tough for Lisa and me. It was hard to figure out where the father began and the boss ended. I think that one of the greatest things for our marriage was when we actually moved to the Dallas-Ft. Worth area.

LISA: Now, the in-laws for Ed and for me are very important. Our parents are huge. When we first relocated to Dallas and went to buy our house, we strongly valued the opinion of our parents. We listened to some of their advice, but we still had plenty of decisions to tough out on our own.

ED: It's funny; neither set of parents liked the choice we made in that first home in Dallas. They thought it was too old, that we would have to pay too much for repairs.

LISA: We valued their opinion. However, our decision was based on our prayer time together, and on our communication with each other. One of the unhealthiest reactions you can have is running to mama or papa rather than looking to your spouse.

Q: *How would you advise people to deal with the in-laws when they pressure their adult children to spend the holidays with them?*

LISA: For us, holidays are kind of tough. For Easter, we are here for our church services. For Christmas, it is the same situation. We made a decision early on to spend the holidays in a way that is best for our family.

Our children enjoy having traditions in our home, so we do everything here and invite the parents to come see us. That works out great. There have been times when we have spent Christmas at their homes, but, for the most part, it is our deal. We definitely want our children's grandparents to be a big part of their lives. Occasionally we will travel to Houston for Thanksgiving.

ED: We try to spend the big holidays, (Christmas being the biggest) at home. And then after Christmas, if we want to go see the extended family, we'll do that.

———

Q: Statistics show that more than fifty percent of marriages end in divorce. What would you have to say about divorce, especially as it relates to those in the church who have gone through or are considering a divorce?

ED: Well, divorce is neither the unpardonable, nor the unforgivable sin. Let me say that, first of all. We serve a God of the second chance. I know many people who have gone through the devastation of divorce, and there is a light at the end of the tunnel.

God's ideal is for one man and one woman to get married

and stay married until they die. However, the Bible does mention three grounds for divorce, which I've already outlined in the previous chapter. The first would be when a divorce occurs prior to belief in Christ; the second, adultery; and the third, desertion. Even so, these are given as a last resort after we have done everything possible to save the marriage.

These biblical grounds for divorce have various nuances. And, if you want to delve more into that, there are some great Christian books you can read for more detailed information on this issue. I would also encourage you to ask your church or pastor for a referral to a good, biblically-based, Christian counselor who can help clarify this issue.

My heart goes out to divorced men and women. I want to minister to their needs. For the most part, no matter how high the price, it is important to try to make the marriage work since the price of divorce is higher. I can think of maybe nine to ten cases over the years where that wouldn't have been true, but there are thousands of others where the marriage could have been salvaged.

> FOR THE MOST PART, NO MATTER HOW HIGH THE PRICE, IT IS IMPORTANT TO TRY TO MAKE THE MARRIAGE WORK SINCE THE PRICE OF DIVORCE IS HIGHER.

LISA: And those several he is mentioning are cases where one spouse was very abusive, was in prison for long standing drug abuse, or some other extreme situation.

ED: But I would say to those who are divorced that you can use your experiences, what you learned from the first marriage, and apply that in your second marriage. You can do the next marriage God's way.

That is why we wrote this book and why we have resources available at our church, as well as numerous classes and seminars about marriage. So, get involved in your church, find the help you need, and do it God's way.

LISA: An important thing to consider before heading to divorce is the sacrifice God made for all of us. If you are in a situation where things are very rocky and divorce looks imminent, think about the price that God paid when our sin separated us from Him, and our relationship with Him was severed. God paid the ultimate price through His son, Jesus Christ to reconcile us. He sent His only Son to die on the cross so that we could be totally restored.

When you consider what God did for our relationship with him, why wouldn't we work harder to give our marriage another chance?

Whether you were married on a hillside in Maui or a stained-glass church in the city, when you said "I Do", it was a covenant before God. And God does not take lightly the breaking of the covenant.

We live in a very disposable society, a quick fix society, and oftentimes, that tends to be the pull. But I pray that you will consider what God has done for you and decide to work harder to give the relationship every opportunity. Today is a new day. It can be a new day in your relationship.

ED: I read that most divorces occur in the first two years of marriage. What that tells me is that during the early years of adjustment, conflict was not handled properly. When you don't crash through those quitting points which we all face, you end up deciding to bail out.

What happens is that you find yourself in a repetitive cycle where the same kind of junk ends up surfacing in the next marriage and the next marriage and the next marriage.

———

Q: Looking back over your marriage, what was one of the toughest times you lived through and how did you get through it?

ED: I would say the first twenty-four months were tough; and also, going from two children to four children when the twins were born was a big adjustment. At that time, we were building our new church complex in Grapevine, Texas, and were still holding four services a weekend in rented facilities. That was a taxing time to say the least.

LISA: Referring to the time when our twins were born, we experienced mounting pressure from all fronts. When this kind of pressure is going on, expect it to carry over to your marital relationship too. You have to do things to safeguard your relationship.

One of the biggest problems we faced was not fighting fair. When arguments came up and conflict arose, we did not use those biblical boundaries that keep the conflict in a positive light.

That sounds a little strange, but conflict can be a very positive thing for your relationship. Back then, though, we tended to name call and compare. Ed is a great imitator and he would throw that in the mix, and I have a strong capacity to get historical with him, remembering every past failure he has committed in our marriage. Needless to say, we weren't exactly fighting fairly!

These conflicts were negative, and they didn't do anything to elevate our relationship. If anything, they tore his self-esteem down and my self-esteem down. Conflict can be beneficial if you fight fairly and come to a resolution. Once this happens, your relationship is taken to a higher level.

Also, Ed and I believe that some arguing needs to be done before the children. Now, that might sound strange, but if done properly, you are modeling conflict resolution for your children.

Our children do see us disagree from time to time. We do not get into heated battles in front of our children, but they do know that we hold varying opinions on certain things. They see Ed's leadership role and how he listens to my opinions. They also see how forgiveness works in a relationship.

If you argue in front of your children, but do not resolve it in front of them, I would consider that unhealthy. But, if you show forgiveness and resolution, you are modeling for them how to handle the issues on the playground and how to handle tense times with their friends. Most importantly, you are showing them how to handle conflict in their future marriage relationship.

———

Q: *In the chapter on sex builders and sex busters, you talked about the husband and wife fulfilling each other's sexual needs. How often should a couple have sex?*

ED: I think about 1 Corinthians 7, where it says that we should not deprive one another except when we mutually agree for a time of prayer. We try to live that out. I think couples that try to hit some national average, or whatever, are missing the point.

We are to satisfy each other creatively, intentionally, strategically, and lovingly. So when one is in the mood and one is not, (and that is often the norm) the one with the lesser desire should fulfill his or her duty to the spouse in an enthusiastic way.

Not just, "Wait; you mean again tonight?" Giving of ourselves sexually is part of our discipleship. Some day we will be held accountable before God on how we served our spouse sexually.

When one partner wants to say no for whatever reason, it should be no with an appointment. There are some great books on human sexuality written by Christian authors. "The Gift Of Sex," (Clifford Penner) and "Intended For Pleasure" (Ed Wheat) are just two of them. There are many others. I believe they will help answer this and many other questions about sex in greater detail.

———

Q: *How do you keep the fires of intimacy burning in marriage?*

LISA: Well, we really work hard at understanding, knowing and satisfying the other's needs. When you are talking about intimacy in marriage, there are certain physical needs that you need to discuss. But we have found that romance is a huge part of it.

What happens in the bedroom does not start there. It is a whole package deal, which includes valuing one another, what we say to one another, and our date night. We have common interests and we enjoy our relationship.

Ed and I have a lot of fun together. I think creativity definitely plays a huge role. We both love the excitement that comes from a new dining, or entertainment adventure.

The key is to mix it up. Don't always go to the same places. Try going your whole date night with just $10. Recreate the events of your dating relationship.

We laugh a lot together. We enjoy going places together. Sometimes it means I need to do some things for Ed that I wouldn't naturally do. Other times, Ed will compromise for my benefit. We enjoy animals, Vietnamese food, and movies. We are also both athletic and enjoy sports. I don't really get into fly-fishing, but he loves it. I can communicate how much I value Ed by watching fly-fishing shows with him or bringing a new video home regarding fly-fishing techniques.

Ed is not into the theater as much as I am, but sometimes we will go see a play or musical together. Going to antique stores is not his favorite thing to do, but I like it. So we do things like that for each other.

ED: We try to appreciate each other's interests and that helps. I agree that creativity is huge. We do a lot of fun stuff together, and are always trying new things.

When we have those common bonds and experiences together outside the bedroom, and communicate very openly about likes and dislikes in the bedroom, it keeps the house hot.

———

Q: Ed, you talk often about the importance of the church in every Christ follower's life. How important has the church been in your marriage?

ED: Well, even if we were not in the ministry, we would still reap the marital benefits of being connected to a local church. The Christians in the New Testament were always connected to a local church. What I mean by connected is they came together corporately, but also met in small groups.

Lisa and I have some friends in our church family that we just love. We share challenges and victories. We are after the same goal, to glorify Christ in our marriage. It is important to expose your relationship to others who have common values. That is why we talk on and on in our church about our small groups, called HomeTeams.

If you are a couple or a single adult, and you are not involved in a small group in your church, you need to get involved in the lives of other believers. This is a time where you can learn from the Bible and discuss some issues that are applicable to whatever stage of life you are in. You also deepen your walk by getting to know other couples on a more intimate level. This will keep you accountable with couples who share your beliefs, and goals.

I would definitely say that without the church, our marriage would only be a four out of ten, rather than the nine or ten it is today.

LISA: The church has taught us, through the study of Scripture, how to have a daily walk with the Lord individually. We do not have a set time in our home when we open the Bible and have devotions together. Ed studies all week and he has his personal quiet time. I have my personal time of study early in the morning. Then, as a family, we often pray openly and read Scripture before dinner. But I wouldn't say that nightly family devotions are the rule for us.

We are also very proactive about teaching our children by capturing teachable moments. For instance, while carpooling one day, I noticed that a critical conversation was going on in the car regarding some students in their classes and various teachers. I shared with them what I had been reading in the Bible regarding the power of words and the impact that negative words have on us. So, the influence of the church and the Holy Spirit is a daily flow for us.

Of course, when we pray with our children before they go to bed, we talk to them during this time about the issues they are dealing with.

The great thing about the church is that we can find others connected to Christ who share the same goals we do in our marriage, and in the way they raise their children. That is enormously helpful.

A FINAL THOUGHT FROM ED YOUNG:

As the pastor of a growing church, and having been in the ministry for many years, I cannot stress enough to each one who is reading this book the importance of the local church in the life of your marriage.

We intentionally ended the book with this critical issue, because none of what we have talked about will be possible without the support of a local body of believers. The mutual encouragement, the service from and to others, the biblical accountability, and so many other aspects of the church are vitally important as you build and maintain your lives together.

And, even more fundamental, is the impact that the church will make on the lives of your children, now and forever.

If you don't take anything else away from this book, I would urge you to find a church and get involved. I know it can be uncomfortable at first, but the effort is well worth the eternal rewards.

Certainly, if you live in the Dallas/Fort Worth area, I would welcome you to visit Fellowship Church. We'd love for you to discover God in a creative and dynamic environment, where you can learn in very practical ways more about what it means to be a Christ-follower and enjoy a creative and lasting marriage.

Other books by Ed Young available on EdYoung.com or CreativePastors.com:

You!
The Journey to the Center of Your Worth

The answer to reaching your greatest potential lies in this God-centered approach to the journey to the center of your worth. In this meaningful book, you will quickly discover that you are God's treasure—divinely loved, cherished, and chosen—and encounter a whole new view of YOU!

High Definition Living
Bringing Clarity to Your Life's Mission

Ed Young has developed a high-octane approach to discovering your leadership potential in his book, High Definition Living: Bringing Clarity to Your Life's Mission. In High Definition Living, Young goes a step further by taking the model and making it practical. Our mission as people of God is to make an impact, to be salt and light in the world around us, within our circle of influence. High Definition Living illustrates how anyone can become a C.E.O: a person of Creativity, Enthusiasm and Organization.

Kid CEO
How to Keep Your Children From Running Your Life

Through a thought-provoking yet entertaining analysis of contemporary family dynamics, Ed Young challenges parents to reclaim their leadership role and explains why marriage must take first priority in the home.

Rating Your Dating While Waiting for Mating

Being single in today's world can be a springboard toward fulfilling, lifelong relationships and rewarding commitments, or it can be a downward spiral into the most destructive time of a person's life. So much in life comes down to our crossroad choices as a single. In this surprisingly candid book, Ed teaches on four critical dating issues to help singles date and choose a mate God's way.

Know Fear
Facing Life's Six Most Common Phobias

Know Fear specifically addresses six common fears: helplessness, the future, commitment, failure, loneliness, and death. And then shows us, ironically, that it is through fear—a proper understanding of the fear of God—that we are able to get back on track. Psalm 111:10 reads, "The fear of the Lord is the beginning of wisdom." A whole new perspective on life awaits those who are willing to face life's fears.

These and many other series are available on CD and DVD at EdYoung.com or CreativePastors.com:

Who's Kidding Who?

Has parental authority become the punch line of a national joke? Sadly, we have allowed a cynical society to kid us into thinking that parenting is laughable and obsolete. Well, Ed Young's not kidding when he says, "Parenting is no joke!" As we take a serious look at God's design for the family, we'll find out that it is possible to restore order and sanity to the home.

I Don't

Every married couple says two words that will change their lives forever: "I Do." But before the "I Dos," we need to remember the "I Don'ts." In this contemporary series on relationships, Ed Young considers the things we don't do before and after marriage that make all the difference in the lasting impact of the marital vows.

Men and Women

So God created man in his own image, in the image of God he created him; male and female he created them - Genesis 1:27. Unquestionably, there has been some serious gender confusion over the last several decades. Most of us don't really understand who we are as men and women. In this timely series, Ed Young teaches that God can rescue and refurbish our true masculinity and femininity based on the perfect character of Jesus Christ.

RPMs: Recognizing Potential Mates

Whether you're a single adult, a student, or a parent, this creatively driven series of talks will provide foundational principles on how to date and select a mate God's way. We're going to cruise past the cultural myths and embark on a supercharged ride to the ultimate relational destination.

Just Lust

Men and women alike, no one escapes its insidious influence. God calls it the lust of the flesh and it has the power to enslave and destroy everyone it touches. In this hard-hitting series of talks, Ed Young provides a strategy for spiritual survival in a culture of lust.